D0554711

# The Modern Latin
# American Novel

# Twayne's Critical History of the Novel

## Herbert Sussman, Series Editor
*Northeastern University*

# The Modern Latin American Novel

## Raymond Leslie Williams
*University of California, Riverside*

Twayne Publishers
An Imprint of Simon & Schuster Macmillan
New York

Prentice Hall International
London • Mexico City • New Delhi • Singapore • Sydney • Toronto

Twayne's Critical History of the Novel Series

*The Modern Latin American Novel*
Raymond Leslie Williams

Twayne Publishers
An Imprint of Simon & Schuster Macmillan
1633 Broadway
New York, New York 10019

**Library of Congress Cataloging-in-Publication Data**

Williams, Raymond L.
    The modern Latin American novel / Raymond Leslie Williams.
        p.   cm. — (Twayne's critical history of the novel)
    Includes bibliographical references and index.
    ISBN 0-8057-1655-6 (alk. paper)
        1. Latin American fiction—20th century—History and criticism.
    I. Title.   II. Series.
    PQ7082.N7W548   1998
    863—dc21                                                    98-25148
                                                                    CIP

This paper meets the requirements of ANSI/NISO
Z3948–1992 (Permanence of Paper).

10 9 8 7 6 5 4 3

Printed in the United States of America

*For Warren, Fritz,
Ken, and Oliver*

# Contents

# Preface

The modern novel in Latin America has been in the spotlight of an international reading public since the 1960s. Writers such as Nobel laureates Gabriel García Márquez, Miguel Angel Asturias, and Pablo Neruda have done much to place Latin American writing at the forefront of world literature. Latin American literature, however, belongs to a tradition that precedes these four writers and the 1960s. In the present volume, I introduce and analyze the novel in Latin America since the rise of modernist fiction in the region in the mid-1940s.

In part 1 "The Rise of the Modernist Novel (1945–1957)," I review modernist fiction since the 1940s, with the main focus on the 12-year period after 1945. After an introductory chapter on modernist fiction in Latin America, I continue with chapters on the fiction of the Guatemalan Miguel Angel Asturias (chapter 2), the Mexican Agustín Yáñez (chapter 3), and the Cuban Alejo Carpentier (chapter 4). In chapter 5, I discuss the novels of two writers from the River Plate region, the Argentine Leopoldo Marechal and the Uruguayan Juan Carlos Onetti. Chapter 6 deals with the fiction of four modernist writers from Brazil.

Part 2 deals with the modernist Boom, with the main focus on the novelistic production that appeared from 1958 to 1967. After an introduction to the Boom (chapter 7), I cover the novels of Carlos Fuentes (chapter 8), Julio Cortázar (chapter 9), Mario Vargas Llosa (chapter 10), and Gabriel García Márquez (chapter 11). Chapter 12 deals with four accomplished writers of this period who were not part of the Boom: the Chilean José Donoso, the Brazilians Clarice Lispector and João Guimarães Rosa, and the Venezuelan Salvador Garmendia.

In part 3, "The Postmodern Novel," I discuss the most innovative fiction to appear in the region since 1968. After an introduction to postmodern fiction in Latin America, I provide an overview of postmodern fiction in South America (chapter 14) and in Mexico and the

Caribbean (chapter 15). In chapter 16, I offer concluding remarks about the modern and postmodern novel in Latin America as well as about a recent variant on the postmodern that I identify as the postnational novel.

Several recent studies on the modern novel in Latin America have been exceptionally valuable for this book. Most important, I have drawn from John S. Brushwood's landmark book *The Spanish American Novel: A Twentieth Century Survey* (1975), which provides an analytical overview of the Spanish American novel from 1900 to 1970. Naomi Lindstrom's well-informed study *Twentieth-Century Spanish American Fiction* (1994) was also quite useful in the research for the present book. Conceptually, this volume also represents, in some ways, a continuation of studies that I had initiated with *The Colombian Novel: 1844–1987* (1991) and *The Postmodern Novel in Latin America* (1995).

Throughout the book, English titles are given for novels that have been translated into English, followed by the date of the original publication in Spanish. When novels have not been translated, I use the Spanish title, followed by my English translation of it in parentheses.

The completion of this book was possible only with the support of certain individuals as well as the generous editing work of several colleagues. The timely support of my wife, Pamela, and the dean of the College of Humanities, Arts and Social Sciences at the University of California, Riverside, Carlos Vélez Ibáñez, were essential to this book's completion in the autumn of 1997. Professors John S. Brushwood, William Megenney, George McMurray, and Donald Schmidt provided valuable editorial suggestions. I particularly appreciate the improvements to the manuscript suggested by Professor Herb Sussman. Nevertheless, the final content of this study is mine, as are any errors of judgment or fact.

# Chronology

1945    Adolfo Bioy Casares, *Plan de evasión*. Enrique Amorim, *El asesino desvelado*.

1946    Augusto Céspedes, *Metal del diablo*. Miguel Angel Asturias, *El Señor Presidente*. Jorge Amado, *Seara vermelha*.

1947    Agustín Yáñez, *The Edge of the Storm*. Graciliano Ramos, *Insônia*.

1948    Leopoldo Marechal, *Adán Buenosayres*. Ernesto Sábato, *The Tunnel*. José Lins do Rêgo, *Eurídice*.

1949    Alejo Carpentier, *The Kingdom of This World*. Miguel Angel Asturias, *Men of Maíze*. Yolanda Oreamuno, *La ruta de su evasión*.

1950    Miguel Angel Asturias, *Strong Wind*. Juan Carlos Onetti, *The Brief Life*. Ramón Díaz Sánchez, *Cumboto*.

1952    Eduardo Caballero Calderón, *El cristo de espaldas*.

1953    Alejo Carpentier, *The Lost Steps*.

1954    Juan Carlos Onetti, *Los adioses*. Jorge Amado, *Os subterrâneos da liberdade*. Miguel Angel Asturias, *The Green Pope*.

1955    David Viñas, *Cayó sobre su rostro*. Gabriel García Márquez, *Leafstorm*. Juan Rulfo, *Pedro Páramo*. Antonio Di Benedetto, *El pentágono*. Miguel Otero Silva, *Casas muertas*.

1956    Miguel Angel Asturias, *Weekend in Guatemala*. João Guimarães Rosa, *The Devil to Pay in the Backlands*.

1957    José Donoso, *Coronation*. Alejo Carpentier, *El acoso*. Rosario Castellanos, *Balún Canán*.

1958    Carlos Fuentes, *Where the Air Is Clear*. José María Arguedas, *Los ríos profundos*. Jorge Amado, *Gabriela, Clove and Cinnamon*. Julio Cortázar, *The Winners*.

1959    Agustín Yáñez, *La creación*. Augusto Roa Bastos, *Hijo de hombre*. Juan Carlos Onetti, *Una tumba sin nombre*. Salvador Garmendia, *Los pequeños seres*.

1960    Julio Cortázar, *Los premios*. Miguel Angel Asturias, *The Eyes of the Interred*. Sergio Galindo, *The Precipice*. Carlos Fuentes, *The Good Conscience*. Agustín Yáñez, *La tierra pródiga*. Julio

Ramón Ribeyro, *Crónica de San Gabriel.* Juan Carlos Onetti, *La casa de la desgracia.* Agustín Yáñez, *Ojerosa y pintada.* Clarice Lispector, *Family Ties.*

1961    Gabriel García Márquez, *No One Writes to the Colonel.* Juan Carlos Onetti, *The Shipyard.* Salvador Garmendia, *Los habitantes.*

1962    Ernesto Sábato, *On Heroes and Tombs.* Alvaro Cepeda Zamudio, *La casa grande.* Gabriel García Márquez, *In Evil Hour.* Héctor Rojas Herazo, *Respirando el verano.* Alejo Carpentier, *Explosion in a Cathedral.* Carlos Fuentes, *The Death of Artemio Cruz.* Carlos Fuentes, *Aura.* Agustín Yáñez, *Las tierras flacas.* Rosario Castellanos, *Oficio de tinieblas.*

1963    Julio Cortázar, *Hopscotch.* Severo Sarduy, *Gestos.* Miguel Angel Asturias, *Mulata.* Mario Vargas Llosa, *The Time of the Hero.*

1964    Manauel Zapata Olivella, *A Saint Is Born in Chimá.* Manuel Mejía Vallejo, *El día señalado.* Juan Carlos Onetti, *Juntacadáveres.* Salvador Garmendia, *Día de ceniza.*

1965    Gustavo Sainz, *Gazapo.* Salvador Elizondo, *Farabeuf.* Mario Vargas Llosa, *The Green House.* Julio Ramón Ribeyro, *Los geniecillos dominicales.* José Balza, *Marzo anterior.*

1966    José Donoso, *This Sunday.* José Donoso, *Hell Has No Limits.* José Lezama Lima, *Paradiso.* José Agustín, *De perfil.*

1967    Néstor Sánchez, *Siberia Blues.* Gabriel García Márquez, *One Hundred Years of Solitude.* Guillermo Cabrera Infante, *Three Trapped Tigers.* Carlos Fuentes, *A Change of Skin.* Carlos Fuentes, *Holy Place.* José Emilio Pacheco, *You Will Die in a Distant Land.* Clarice Lispector, *The Apple in the Dark.*

1968    Julio Cortázar, *62: A Model Kit.* Manuel Puig, *Betrayed by Rita Hayworth.* Jorge Guzmán, *Job-Boj.* Alberto Duque López, *Mateo el flautista.* José Agustín, *Inventado que sueño.* Salvador Elizondo, *El hipogeo secreto.* Francisco Massiani, *Piedra de mar.* Salvador Garmendia, *La mala vida.* Adriano González León, *País portátil.* Héctor Libertella, *El camino de los hiperbóreos.* José Balza, *Largo.*

1969    Manuel Puig, *Heartbreak Tango.* Gustavo Sainz, *Obsesivos días circulares.* Carlos Fuentes, *Birthday.* Mario Vargas Llosa,

1991    Diamela Eltit, *Sacred Cow*. Antonio Ostornol, *Los años de la serpiente*. Alberto Fuguet, *Mala onda*. Brianda Domecq, *Once días . . . y algo más*. Carmen Boullosa, *They're Cows, We're Pigs*.

1992    Ricardo Piglia, *La ciudad ausente*.

1993    Héctor Libertella, *Las sagradas escrituras*. Ignacio Solares, *El gran elector*. Carmen Boullosa, *La milagrosa*. Mario Vargas Llosa, *Death in the Andes*.

1994    Héctor Abad Faciolince, *The Joy of Being Awake*. Carlos Fuentes, *Diana, the Goddess Who Hunts Alone*.

1995    Darío Jaramillo Agudelo, *Cartas cruzadas*.

# PART 1

# THE RISE OF THE MODERNIST NOVEL

# 1

# *Introduction to Modernist Fiction in Latin America (1945–1957)*

For many foreign readers of the fiction of Latin America, the rise of Gabriel García Márquez, Carlos Fuentes, Mario Vargas Llosa, and Julio Cortázar in the 1960s, followed by the attendant popularity of Isabel Allende and Laura Esquivel, signaled the birth of an innovative and attractive type of writing. In reality, the roots of modernist fiction in this region originated in the 1940s with the short fiction of Jorge Luis Borges and the novels of the first generation of modernist writers, which included the Guatemalan Miguel Angel Asturias, the Cuban Alejo Carpentier, the Mexican Agustín Yáñez, the Argentine Leopoldo Marechal, and the Brazilians Graciliano Ramos, Rachel de Queiroz, Jorge Amado, and José Lins do Rêgo.[1] Two decades later, the exceptional quality of fiction written in Latin America was internationally recognized; with this recognition and translation, what became universally known as the Boom of Latin American fiction of the 1960s and the popularity of magic realism were born.

The generation of Asturias and Carpentier had been well acquainted with European modernist writing and theory since the 1920s. Asturias went to Europe in 1923, studying the Mayan collection at the British Museum and then Mayan mythology at the Sorbonne. He also became acquainted with the most prominent French surrealists, such as Paul Éluard and André Breton, as well as with European avant-garde writing in general. He was particularly attracted to expressionism. While in Paris, Asturias worked on translations and his own creative writing and came to know the Peruvian poet César Vallejo, the Venezuelan writer Arturo Uslar Pietri, and Carpentier.

The poet Robert Desnos had helped Carpentier escape political repression in Cuba and find exile in Paris. In Europe, Carpentier became deeply engaged in European and Latin American culture of the moment and participated in the literary circles of Louis Aragon, Tristan Tzara, and Paul Éluard.

Asturias, Carpentier, Borges, and their entire generation, then, were well acquainted with the basic tenets of European modernism and were fully committed to the proposition of writing a modernist fiction in Latin America. In Brazil, modernism was officially launched in 1922 with the Semana de Arte Moderna, a celebration of the avant-garde that had enduring repercussions. Like Anglo-American modernism, the new fiction of Latin America had progressively less to do with the world of ideas or substances that may be objectively known in themselves than with the fictionalization and understanding of the world that can be known and experienced only through individual consciousness.[2] In *El Señor Presidente* (1946), for example, Asturias filtered the image of a dictator through the individual consciousness of several characters, using a series of stratagems well known in Anglo-American modernism.

The narrative strategies appropriated by Asturias and other Latin American modernists could be easily associated with numerous European and American fiction writers, but those with the most impact on the novelists were Faulkner, Proust, and Dos Passos. (The presence of Joyce was felt later in Latin America and has been evident in postmodern writing since the late 1960s and 1970s.)[3] These stratagems included the use of interior monologues, stream of consciousness, fragmentation, varying narrative points of view, neologisms, innovative narrative structures, and frequent lack of causality. Many young Latin American intellectuals had read Proust, and it was common practice for them to structure the time of their novels around a series of associations with an object, thus enacting Proust's use of the now-famous madeleine cookie in *A la recherche du temps perdu*.

Borges was neither a radical nor a flashy innovator in terms of form. Rather, he was a more subtle and profound modernizing force. His major contribution to this first generation of Latin American modernists was his reaffirmation of the right of invention.[4] Seemingly an obvious right for novelists in Europe and the United States, pure invention had been under attack (and fallen into disrepute) by more realist, more nationalist, and often more parochial Latin American intellectuals in the 1920s and 1930s. While Asturias, Carpentier, and Borges were in Europe and engaged in the new avant-garde movements, the cultural wars in Latin America were being lost to the nationalists, who argued forcefully that the new avant-garde movements were "inappropriate" forms of literature for their respective nations and for Latin America.[5] These nationalists, who promoted a type of New Worldism usually identified in Spanish as *criollismo,* predominated in Spanish America during the 1920s and 1930s. The exception, of course, was Brazil, where modernist writing was much more in vogue in the 1920s.

Given the local circumstances, Borges's reaffirmation of the right of invention was a revolution. His volumes of short stories *El jardín de los senderos que se bifurcan* (1941, The garden of the forking path,) and *Ficciones* (1944, Ficciones) suggested new and virtually unknown paths for Latin American writers. Stories such as "The Secret Miracle" problematized time in ways that few Latin American writers had dared to explore in fiction. This same story and many others by Borges contained metafictional qualities that invited readers to think of literature itself as a subject for fiction, a topic considered irrelevant by the dominant nationalists—who ferociously defended novels dealing with "the land."[6] Subjective time and space explored by modernist writing in general, however, was a common experience for readers of *Ficciones.*

Borges also wrote a few fictions that seemingly had no story at all; pieces such as "Pierre Menard, Author of the *Quixote*" and "The Library of Babel" offered virtually none of the "action" of Borges's realist and modernist predecessors. This type of writing, which blurred the line between fiction and essay, was a liberation for Latin America's modernist writers; Borges's "ficciones" were foundational texts for Latin America's later postmodern writers (see chaps. 13 and 14).[7] By making his typical referents not geography but esoteric texts of literature, philosophy, and theology, Borges opened the door for a multiplicity of fictional practices in the 1940s and 1950s. His witty language, novel use of detail, and numerous erudite (as well as pseudoerudite) references have already left their mark on several generations of Latin American fiction writers.

The new modernist fiction in Latin America, written under the sign of Borges, Faulkner, Proust, Dos Passos, and Kafka, was published not only by Asturias, Carpentier, Yáñez, Marechal, Graciliano Ramos, Rachel de Queiroz, Jorge Amado, and José Lins do Rêgo in the 1940s and 1950s but also by lesser-known writers who, in some cases, were equally talented. One of the most gifted of these figures was the Mexican Juan Rulfo, who published only one novel, *Pedro*

*Páramo* (1955, Pedro Páramo). Argentina's David Viñas, Uruguay's Antonio Di Benedetto, and Colombia's Gabriel García Márquez wrote patently Faulknerian novels in the 1950s. Two women writers, the Mexican Rosario Castellanos and the Costa Rican Yolanda Oreamuno, published modernist fiction during this period, and their work certainly merited much more recognition than it ever received. The Chilean José Donoso, who later became an insider of the Boom, authored his first novel, *Coronation*, in 1957. Other noteworthy modernist novels that appeared in the 1940s and 1950s were written by the Colombian Eduardo Caballero Calderón, the Venezuelans Miguel Otero Silva and Ramón Díaz Sánchez, and the Argentine Ernesto Sábato.

The most unequivocal indicator of the rise of the new modernist novel in Latin America was the appearance in successive years of Asturias's *El Señor Presidente* (1946), Yáñez's *Al filo del agua* (1947, The edge of the storm), Ramos's *Insônia* (stories, 1947, Insomnia), Marechal's *Adán Buenosayres* (1948, Adán Buenosayres), and Carpentier's *The Kingdom of This World* (1949). The publication of this fiction confirmed a dramatic transformation of the general direction of the Latin American novel. In *El Señor Presidente,* Asturias portrayed the terror of a classic Latin American dictatorship through multiple points of view. Yáñez was even more radical with his use of multiple points of view and a fragmented structure. Marechal invented multiple texts in *Adán Buenosayres.*

Many Latin American writers of this period were intrigued by the possibilities Faulknerian narrative strategies offered for telling the stories of their respective regions. García Márquez, Viñas, Di Benedetto, and Rulfo were deeply engaged in the writings of Faulkner in the 1950s and produced superbly constructed modernist texts in the Faulknerian mode: *Leafstorm* (1955) by García Márquez, *Cayó sobre su rostro* (1955) by Viñas, *El pentágono* (1955) by Di Benedetto, and *Pedro Páramo* (1955) by Rulfo. García Márquez had read *As I Lay Dying* with acuity and used three different narrators to tell the story of fictional Macondo—his Yoknapatawpha County—from 1903 to 1928 in *Leafstorm*. The novel is set in a home where a doctor has committed suicide. The three narrators are a young boy, his mother, and his grandfather. The novel weaves through a 25-year time period, with narrative fragments that move back in time and through different levels of reality. García Márquez already was a master craftsman in the 1950s; Viñas also was a deft technician in *Cayó sobre su rostro*, a novel in which the chapters alternate between the past and the present, but both novels suggest ways in which the past affects the present. It is a historical novel that debunks some of Argentina's nineteenth-century military leaders who had been considered national heroes. Di Benedetto's *El pentágono* is a novel of a love relationship among five characters, and the author's expert use of narrative point of view is just as fine-tuned as García Márquez's and Viñas's.

Writers such as García Márquez, Viñas, and Di Benedetto, like Faulkner, use a specific region to create a more universal human experience than had generally been the case for Latin American regionalists before the 1940s. This new type of regionalism, which one informed critic has identified as transcendent regionalism, is the type of fiction also cultivated by Juan Rulfo.[8] A reader of Faulkner, Rulfo had published a volume of well-constructed Faulknerian stories set in rural Mexico, *El llano en llamas* (1953), before the appearance of one of the most prestigious modernist novels of Latin America, *Pedro Páramo*. It is a brief and fragmented novel that relates the story of a landowner and local boss—a *cacique*—of the sort known throughout Latin America. As the reader progresses through the initial fragments of *Pedro Páramo*, it becomes apparent after approximately 60 pages that all the characters in the disturbing town of Comala are, in fact, deceased. The novel also moves the reader unexpectedly to a series of fragments that weave through different (and unidentified) periods in the past narrated by frequently unidentified characters. The multiple levels of the narrative structure correspond to multiple thematic levels, and unity is achieved by the systematic use of certain images, such as water, which always corresponds to a move to the past. *Pedro Páramo* is both a local story and a universal story of frustrated love, repression, and solitude.

Authors such as José Donoso, Miguel Otero Silva, and Ramón Díaz Sánchez published modernist novels that were less flashy in narrative technique. In his first novel, *Coronación*, Donoso employed interior monologues to characterize a protagonist, an aging Chilean oligarch, who narrates a story of frustrated human relationships. Otero Silva also uses soft touches of narrative technique, such as special syntactical structures and certain stylistic devices to characterize the people in a decadent town. His *Casas muertas* (1955) is constructed primarily on the basis of extended flashbacks, and the author carefully avoids the potentially obvious symbolism of the decadence surrounding "dead houses." Otero Silva is just as com-

mitted to social justice as he is to subtle narrative technique, but nei-
ther interferes with him or the reader in *Casas muertas*. Díaz
Sánchez's *Cumboto* (1950) is also more subtle than the typical Latin
American novel of social protest written in the 1930s and 1940s.

The Faulknerian novels of transcendent regionalism tended to
offer a broad, muralistic view of society. Some novelists of the
period used less obvious and ambitious strategies to create novels of
the interior dimension, frequently psychological studies of one or
more characters. Ernesto Sábato and Yolanda Oreamuno published
*El túnel* (1948) and *La ruta de su evasión* (1949), respectively; these are
novels of interiorization, works typical of the modernist aesthetic
concern over individual consciousness and, just as typical of the
1950s, novels of existential anguish. Sábato develops philosophical
ideas and a psychological portrayal of love, jealousy, and murder in
*El túnel*, a novel dealing with a protagonist who is profoundly isolated from others. The protagonist in *La ruta de su evasión* is equally
incapable of establishing relationships with others , and also suffers
from existential anguish.

Latin America's venerable tradition of social literature, well represented in *El Señor Presidente*, had numerous manifestations in the
1940s and 1950s; and two of the most successful novels of this type
were Rosario Castellanos's *Balún Canán* (1957) and Eduardo Caballero
Calderón's *El cristo de espaldas* (1952). *Balún Canán* was Rosario Castellanos's first novel set in the southern indigenous region of Chiapas,
Mexico, where she initiated her *indigenista* fiction. In this novel, she
narrates her story through the individual consciousness of a young
girl. The context for *El cristo de espaldas* is the civil war in Colombia in
the 1950s, identified as La Violencia (1948–1956). The novel tells the
story of a parricide in a small town; a son who belongs to one political
party kills his father, who belongs to another.

The major Brazilian novelists of the 1940s and 1950s were social
critics who also hewed to the aesthetics of modernism. Since the
Semana de Arte Moderna in 1922, Brazilian writers have been dedicated to the modernization of Brazilian fiction. One result of this
process was the rise of four important novelists from the northeastern region of Brazil: Graciliano Ramos, Jorge Amado, Rachel de
Queiroz, and José Lins do Rêgo.[9] In general, they were not as enthusiastic about experimenting with narrative technique as were many
novelists writing in Spanish, such as Asturias and Rulfo. Nevertheless, these northeastern writers had read Faulkner and produced

novels of transcendent regionalism comparable in many ways to the fiction of Faulkner, Rulfo, and the early García Márquez by using an identifiable regionalist base to create universal experience. Of these Brazilian writers, Ramos was the most associated with the new aesthetics of modernism and Faulknerian techniques.

Born in 1892, Ramos was 30 years old at the time of the Semana de Arte Moderna. He was a militant member of the Communist Party who wrote one of the early regionalist and modernist novels, *Caetés* (1933). He was already experimenting with novels of interiorization in the 1930s, a time when the vast majority of Brazilian novelists were using relatively simplistic schemes. Ramos's understanding of literature as linguistic creation rendered him directly comparable to Asturias and Yáñez. Best known for his novel *Barren Lives* (1938), he was translated into Spanish in the 1940s and experimented with narrative technique in his volume of short stories *Insônia* (1947).

Jorge Amado, Rachel de Queiroz, and José Lins do Rêgo were Brazilian modernists who created a substantial body of fiction during this period. The most productive of the group was Amado, whose commitment to social change was so marked during this period that many readers and critics complained that his novels were too laden with ideas and direct political messages. He began publishing fiction in the 1930s and later wrote *Seara vermelha* (1946) and *Os subterrâneos da liberdade* (1954). Rachel de Queiroz brought women characters and women's themes to the forefront of Brazilian culture. She published her major fiction in the 1930s, although a notable second edition of *As Tres Marias* appeared in 1943 and a trilogy of three previously published novels, *Tres Romances* (Three novels), in 1948. Lins do Rêgo also initiated a prolific and successful career as one of Brazil's pioneer modernist novelists in the 1930s. His *Fogo morto* (1943) is one of his most celebrated novels, and *Eurídice* is his first psychological novel of individual consciousness. In most of his fiction, however, Lins do Rêgo presents human beings in conflict with the land, acting within a broad social context.

The Latin American novelists of the 1940s and 1950s were well aware of the basic tenets of modernism, and their understanding of the aesthetics of modernism dramatically transformed Latin American fiction. The beginnings of this revolution in fiction are to be found in the fiction of Borges in the Spanish-speaking regions of Latin America, and in the 1922 Semana de Arte Moderna in Brazil. Like their counterparts in Europe and the United States, these writers searched for new methods to know the world through individual consciousness. Unlike their counterparts, however, many of these Latin American modernists remained somewhat concerned with the world of ideas or substances that could be objectively known—the social realities that had concerned several generations of Latin American writers. Asturias and García Márquez, for example, were experimenting with both individual consciousness and the objective world of social reality. Consequently, the enthusiastic reception of Faulkner by this generation of Latin American writers was understandable, for these novelists found in Faulkner innovative narrative strategies, new methods for exploring individual consciousness, and a hierarchical, traditional society like their own.

With the rise of modernist fiction in Latin America between 1945 and 1957, Latin American novelists were clearly confident of their craftsmanship. These writers deftly handled fragmented narrative structure, varying points of view, and similar techniques. They explored new depths in the reality of the region, penetrating the interior of both the individual and the collectivity. With their writing, these mature and modern novelists reaffirmed their right to create a fiction that not only reproduced reality but also invented it.

# 2

# *The Novels of Miguel Angel Asturias*

After the reaffirmation of the right of invention by Borges in the early 1940s, the first notable novelistic indicator of a new, modernist fiction in Latin America was the appearance of *El Señor Presidente* (1946), a dictator novel by the Guatemalan Miguel Angel Asturias. Given the relatively limited interaction among Latin American writers during the 1940s, this novel was a modernist sign that passed by virtually unnoticed in Latin America. But as *El Señor Presidente* became better known, it was read not only as a political statement but also as an unequivocal aesthetic one that reflected Asturias's contact with expressionism, surrealism, and cubism in the 1920s. Asturias then published a superb novel, *Men of Maize* in 1949, followed by a trilogy of novels in the 1950s, some short fiction, and the novel *Mulata* (1963) before finally receiving much-deserved international recognition with the Nobel Prize for literature in 1967. Most scholars agree that his most accomplished novels are *El Señor Presidente* and *Men of Maize.*

Asturias and Latin American modernists generally refused to accept the divorce between aesthetics and politics that characterized much modernist writing in Europe and the United States. To the contrary, *El Señor Presidente* is an overtly political novel in which Asturias denounces Latin American dictators. The authority figure is a fictionalized version of Manuel Estrada Cabrera, an early-twentieth-century strongman in Guatemala, even though neither Estrada Cabrera nor Guatemala are actually named in the novel. The time frame is roughly the first half of the century. The novel begins with the murder of a military officer, Colonel José Parrales Sonriente, when a deranged person kills him as an instinctual reaction on the street. The dictator, identified only as "the President," uses this death to eliminate two men, a lawyer named Carvajal and General Canales. He has Carvajal arrested, tried in court, and shot. He plans to have Miguel Cara de Angel persuade Canales to flee his home at night in

11

order to have him shot. Cara de Angel, however, creates an escape scheme that allows the general to escape from his home and into the mountains. Back in the city, Canales's daughter becomes ill, Cara de Angel falls in love with her, and marries her. In the end, he is imprisoned and eventually dies. Despite this outcome and the attendant setbacks for the small group of essentially good individuals in the novel, this piercing denunciation of the ferociously amoral dictator intimates that there is some hope for humanity. For example, students enter the novel near the end, and their new awareness suggests some hope for the future, and the transfiguring power of love is also evident at the end of the novel. The dictator himself appears rarely—only six times—and usually briefly. Rather than operating as a visible character, he is an invisible presence that pervades everything; Estrada Cabrera was a similarly invisible presence in Guatemala.

Scholars have focused considerable attention on *El Señor Presidente*, Asturias's most widely read novel. For one scholar, Asturias achieves universally appreciated effects through the use of language.[1] This scholar also points out that the novel successfully employs both satire and the grotesque, and he considers the grotesque quality its very essence.[2] Naomi Lindstrom considers *El Señor Presidente* the most cosmopolitan and urbane of Asturias's novels and observes how many of the book's features relate directly to the experimentation of the European avant-garde that had been so important for Asturias in the 1920s.[3] She points out perceptively that the word *nightmare* appears frequently, and the novel generates an atmosphere of nightmarish fear and uncertainty. It replicates, Lindstrom explains, certain spatial and temporal distortions characteristic of uneasy dreams.

One informed critic reads *El Señor Presidente* as a cyclic struggle between fertility and destruction.[4] According to this informed interpretation, the president embodies sterility and death, and Cara de Angel represents the generative forces of nature. Richard Callan relates some of the novel's scenes to Mayan mythology but also finds parallels with the mythologies of Babylonia, maintaining that Asturias portrays the Babylonian fertility myth of Tammuz and Ishtar. Callan also finds it appropriate for Asturias to have juxtaposed Babylon, a traditional symbol of corruption and cruelty since biblical times, with Guatemala City or any city suffering a cruel dictatorship.[5]

*El Señor Presidente* opens with an arresting chapter of impressive linguistic texture. Sensory perceptions, especially the sense of smell, dominate the chapter. The novel begins with the narrator's incantation "Alumbra, lumbre de alumbre, Luzbel de piedralumbre!" (referring to lights and the devil) and the sound of church bells. The chapter's initial setting involves a group of beggars on church stairs and a dark street at night; it culminates in the madman's attack and murder of Colonel José Parrales Sonriente. The narrator evokes both Christian and Arabic religious traditions with his language, and after these powerful words of invocation, he closes with a brief final sentence: "Estaba amaneciendo" ["It was daybreak"]. This understatement creates a striking contrast with the powerful language and lengthy sentences of the rest of the chapter.

By creating a strong sense of closure, Asturias demonstrates his sophisticated handling of his craft. In a similar use of a traditional device of fiction, Asturias creates a circular structure in the novel through the presence of a student and a sacristan at the beginning of chapter 2 and in the last chapter. The author employs other time-tested strategies in *El Señor Presidente*, such as the regular use of traditional images of darkness and light.

Nevertheless, Asturias also uses stratagems that connect this novel with expressionism, surrealism, and cubism. George McMurray has pointed out that Asturias relies on expressionistic techniques to suggest irrational mental states in moments of panic.[6] Asturias filters the thoughts of characters whose extreme fear distorts their vision of reality, producing expressionistic effects. The author's exploration of dreams and use of dreamlike imagery (especially the image of a single eye that appears during one dream) connect the novel to surrealism, and the surrealist effects are numerous in this work. With respect to cubism, the presentation of events and characters from numerous angles makes *El Señor Presidente* similar to a cubist painting that offers images of the same object seen from different angles.

*Men of Maíze* is a digressive and elusive modernist work in which Asturias himself has admitted he made no concessions to the reader.[7] The novel's title has its origins in the Mayan belief that the group's flesh was made of corn. The beginning of the novel relates the conflict between the Indians, who strive to maintain their traditional ways of subsistence and living, and outsiders, who attempt to force them to change their ways. The novel is divided into six parts and an epilogue, and the conflict revolves around the cultivation of corn: the outsiders desire to interfere with the Indians' cultivation of corn, even though corn is a sacred form of sustenance for them. The leader of the Indians is Gaspar Ilón, who helps defend the Indians against government soldiers and their leader, Colonel Godoy. Unable to subdue Gaspar Ilón, Colonel Godoy uses a trick: he convinces some of Gaspar's friends to poison him. After Gaspar's death, there is a curse on all those involved with this plot, and within seven years all those involved die a violent death. A later part of the novel, entitled "María Tecún," takes place a generation later and deals with a woman who never actually appears. She is the wife of a blind man, Goyo Yic, who leaves him, taking all the children and most of the family's possessions. In this part of the novel, Goyo Yic travels throughout the countryside in search of her; he travels and searches for years. He is found drunk, accused of criminal acts, and imprisoned.

In the last and most lengthy part, an Indian named Nicho Aquino, who knows none of the main characters of the previous parts of the novel, appears as a mail carrier and becomes the central character. In an elaborate series of events, Nicho's wife disappears, and he eventually goes on a mysterious and magical trip with a type of witch doctor—a *curandero*—the same one who had appeared in the first part of the novel. They enter a cave and see numerous dead people, including Gaspar Ilón. Obviously, this last part should be read as a poetic tale.

Although perhaps not as widely read as *El Señor Presidente, Men of Maíze* has been, nevertheless, widely praised by scholars. For Naomi Lindstrom, *Men of Maíze* is a story of loss.[8] She points out that, by the novel's end, the Indians have suffered a significant erosion of their culture, their vision of the universe and its workings, and their approach to agriculture, seen as a collaborative endeavor between the earth and human collectivity. Gerald Martin considers *Men of Maíze* one of the great novels of the century and a profound medita- tion on the history of Guatemala.[9] He observes that it is one of the few novels dealing with Indians in which the past is *their* past (not the Spanish past), and it is the Spanish invaders who are the prob- lem. Martin also considers *Men of Maíze* the most complete enact- ment of the uprooting of the Indians from their culture and ejection from their homeland.[10]

Richard Callan's reading of *Men of Maíze* emphasizes the truths in the novel's myths and legends, the truths of the psychic need they fulfill.[11] He considers Nicho Aquino the central figure of the novel, the character whose psychic evolution is the heart of the matter.

Using Jungian psychology as the basis for his analysis, Callan observes patterns of sacrifice, rebirth, death, and rebirth in the character of Nicho. He concludes that Nicho's myths are identical in structure and psychological function to those operating in human beings of all times and places.[12] Consequently, he underlines the universality of the novel.

*Men of Maíze* is not only a compelling modernist text but also a masterpiece of the Latin American novel in which Asturias synthesizes both modernist interests and the interests of the traditional folklorist. He incorporates an oral-culture understanding of the world into this novel, using, for example, the repetitions and redundancies that are both typical and absolutely necessary for oral storytelling.[13] As Walter Ong has concluded in his studies of oral cultures, oral tales originating from illiterate societies tend to be close to the "human lifeworld." Consequently, the presence of the "guerrero-pájaro" and "guerrero-cangrejo" in *Men of Maíze* is an indicator that the novel is grounded in an oral-culture mindset.

The language of *Men of Maíze* is a stellar product of an unlikely marriage between modernist experimentation and oral tradition. As a modernist, Asturias exercises the right to experiment with the word and, by repeating syllables within words, he evokes effects of the oral tale. The author's language play is also an attractive feature of the novel, sometimes engendering an intuitive, nonrational communication.

The structure of *Men of Maíze* also corresponds as much to the structures of oral storytelling as to the typical patterns of Western fiction. It does not follow the linear progression of the standard novel, and one critic has observed parallels between this novel and the *Popul Vuh*, the Maya-Quiché sacred text about creation.[14] These parallels account for the novel's discontinuity and non-Western logic. Eschewing Western storytelling practices, Asturias organizes this novel according to different principles.

In the 1950s, Asturias wrote his "banana trilogy" consisting of *Strong Wind* (1950), *The Green Pope* (1954), and *The Eyes of the Interred* (1960). The setting of the three novels is Central America when it was economically and politically dominated by the United Fruit Company. Although not Asturias's most innovative novels in terms of narrative technique, they are grippingly written denunciations of foreign capitalism in Latin America at the same time that they articulate broader concerns.

*Strong Wind* opens with Americans cutting the forests along the Pacific Coast to build a railroad. They contract with local workers to help them confront a hostile nature—heat, wild animals, and ill-ness—and forge the way to their enterprise: a banana plantation. The local workers include Adelaido Lucero, who settles down, remains employed by the Americans, and marries. Having lofty expectations for his sons, Lucero purchases land for them eventually to become independent farmers. Other young men from the highlands become farmers in the region, selling their bananas to the American company, which continually expands its operations. Eventually, friction develops between the company and its laborers. The conflict intensi-fies when the company reduces drastically the price it will pay for bananas. The American president of the company (referred to as *el papa verde*) refuses to take the workers' demands into account.

Asturias' main interest in *Strong Wind* is social inequity. The Americans are stereotypes who describe themselves as "machines," and the Guatemalans are dehumanized by them. Nevertheless, Asturias also inserts an idealistic American couple into the novel; they attempt to form a cooperative with the local workers. In this manner, he avoids limiting the novel strictly to the political and emphasizes certain spiritual and universal concerns. The author conveys once again, as he had in *Men of Maíze*, the deeply human meaning—even joy—in agricultural production and proximity to the land. Consequently, *Strong Wind* should be read as a novel that protests on a spiritual level as well as an economic one.[15]

The second novel of the trilogy, *The Green Pope*, also deals with the arrival of the fruit company to Guatemala, but this time on the Atlantic Coast, where the company purchases the most fertile land for its banana crops. The company hires a young American, Geo Maker Thompson, to take charge of this enterprise. Maker Thompson travels throughout the region, offering high prices to those willing to sell their land and threatening those who are not interested in selling with eviction, for the company has the support of the national armed forces. Most of the locals are deeply attached to their land—for the same spiritual and economic reasons evident in *Strong Wind*—and refuse to sell it. Maker Thompson has them evicted. Although he has a wife and two children, he falls in love with a local woman, Mayarí, who later commits suicide in a ritualistic "marriage" to a river. He attempts to convince the United States government to annex Guatemala as a state, but a political scandal ruins this plan.

The last part of the novel has relatively little to do with Maker Thompson until the end. The Luceros from *Strong Wind* are active in the political and social life of the town. Frictions develop between the Guatemalan and Honduran divisions of the banana company. At the end of *The Green Pope*, Maker Thompson assumes the presidency of the company.

As in *Strong Wind*, in *The Green Pope* Asturias constructs numerous parallels with Mayan mythology and the *Popul Vuh*. Following this myth-based reading, Geo Maker Thompson can be connected to the Mayan creator gods, and other characters can also be associated with various Mayan deities.[16]

The culminating book of the trilogy, *The Eyes of the Interred*, is the most lengthy of the three volumes (over 500 pages). The central character is a new one to the trilogy, Octavio Sansur, an orphan who is reared in an impoverished neighborhood of Guatemala City. He is educated not in schools, but in barbershops, where his reading include the history of the French Revolution, which inspires him. He frees birds from a pet shop while singing *The Marseillaise* and must flee to Panama to avoid police arrest. After several years of exile, he returns to Guatemala to initiate his plans to overthrow the president. When his assassination attempt fails, he flees to the banana plantations and is hidden by the Indians there. After living and working with them, he eventually realizes that the only way to overthrow the dictatorship is to organize the peasants in the rural areas, as well as the workers and professionals in the city. After years of organizing efforts throughout the nation, he gains widespread support both in the country and in the city. Sansur's plan evolves into a program of nonviolent revolution. At the end, the president resigns, and Sansur works to avoid violence or revenge. In this novel's denouement, a new society is emerging in a new spirit of conciliation.

*The Eyes of the Interred* is a mature book in several senses. In it, Asturias's political agenda has matured into a more practical and concrete approach to change. In his previous fiction, he consistently holds a special, mythic view of the land and the Indians' sense of the land. Once again, Asturias demonstrates his ability as a master of the craft of fiction to use language to subtly suggest what characters are like. Sansur is regularly characterized, for example, by images of ashes, underlining his role as the spark of revolutionary fire.

In *Mulata* (1963), Asturias returns to his novelization of oral cultures that had been so well elaborated in *Men of Maíze*. He fictionalizes myths in the context of Native American culture. In this novel, an Indian peasant named Celestino Yumí sells his wife Catalina to a devil figure, Tazol. With his new wealth, Yumí acquires another wife, an attractive mulatta, but whose unbearable behavior eventually makes her a fundamentally negative force. In the end, after learning a moral lesson, Yumí returns to Catalina and the two of them work together to free him from the mulatta.

*Mulata* is something of a traditional Native American oral tale with a moral, as well as a critique of Western materialism. When Catalina disappears with Tazol in a gust of wind, it is the kind of act typically related in an illiterate, oral-culture society. Asturias's free use of invention makes the novel's occasionally improbable and digressive plot entertaining and humorous.

In conclusion, Asturias's novels, from *El Señor Presidente* to *Mulata,* represent a major contribution to modernist fiction in Latin America. His writing shows few direct associations with Borges; nevertheless, Asturias freely exercises the right of invention reaffirmed by Borges with his patently imaginative fiction of the early 1940s. Asturias's right of invention allows him to innovate freely with both language and the use of dreams.

Asturias rejects the divorce between politics and aesthetics that characterized much modernist writing. In addition, he masterfully synthesizes his interests in social change, modernist techniques, and Native American mythology. With respect to the latter, Asturias incorporates many features of oral culture into his fiction, creating effects not common in modern Western writing. These special effects have been identified as "magic realism" by some critics[17]; Asturias was one of the first Latin American writers to produce fiction in this magic-realist vein.

Asturias's modernist techniques—innovative language, multiple points of view, and the like—create a universal experience for his readers. His contact with expressionism, surrealism, and cubism are all evident in his novels. The author also uses myths to create universal experience, constructing parallels between Maya-Quiché mythology and Western mythologies. Asturias's many accomplishments with fiction made him a leading figure in modernist writing in Latin America, an early practitioner of magic realism, and a truly universal novelist who bridged the gap between Borges and the writers of the generation of the Boom.

# 3

# *The Novels of Agustín Yáñez*

Writing in 1966 during the zenith of the Boom, an eminent scholar of Mexican literature described Agustín Yáñez's novel *The Edge of the Storm* as "the best Mexican novel to date."[1] Published in 1947, *The Edge of the Storm* is, indeed, an accomplished modernist novel and a major contribution to the rise of modernist fiction in Mexico and Latin America. Yáñez published four other well-wrought novels: *La creación* (The creation, 1959), *Ojerosa y pintada* (Hollow-eyed and painted, 1960), *La tierra pródiga* (The lush land, 1960), and *The Lean Lands* (1962). Later, he also published *Las vueltas del tiempo* (The return of time, 1975).

Yáñez had been interested in the innovations of European and North American modernism since the 1920s. In Mexico, the voice for the aesthetic and literary agenda of this modernism was the magazine *Contemporáneos,* which was published in the late 1920s and early 1930s. Mexican avant-garde writers such as Jaime Torres Bodet, Salvador Novo, and Xavier Villaurrutia were involved with *Contemporáneos* in order to develop and promote innovative literature in Mexico. Yáñez did not collaborate in *Contemporáneos,* but he did write in a parallel literary review published in Guadalajara, *Bandera de Provincias.* The writers contributing to these journals, including Yáñez, wanted to offer an alternative to the traditionalists and nationalists who conceived of literature primarily as an opportunity to relate realistic accounts of the Mexican Revolution.

Yáñez's short fiction of the 1920s, 1930s, and 1940s, prior to *The Edge of the Storm,* provides some insight into his first novel. In a volume of fiction titled *Los sentidos del aire* (The senses of the air), Yáñez wrote a series of short pieces capturing the atmosphere and essence of the different seasons in rural Jalisco.[2] In *Flor de juegos antiguos* (Flower of ancient games, 1942), he related episodes of traditional life in Guadalajara in the 1930s. In both books, he created scenes similar to those that he developed more fully in *The Edge of the Storm.*

The setting for *The Edge of the Storm* is a small town in the provinces during a year-and-a-half period leading up to the Mexican

Revolution in 1910. The novel begins with a section called the "Acto preparatorio" that sets the tone for the novel and the ambiance of the town. This section presents a series of sense impressions and a static vision of the town. The next chapter introduces four characters, each of whom suffers anguish and frustrations contemplated at night. The third chapter moves rapidly from one character to another, introducing the village priest, Don Dionisio Martínez, in the process. The chapter makes it apparent how the traditions and customs of the Catholic Church dominate all aspects of life in the town. But as the novel progresses, it is also increasingly evident that Don Dionisio and the Church are losing influence among the townsfolk. Seminary students return with attractive stories of life beyond this traditional village. "Northerners" return from their jobs in the United States with more anecdotes of modern life and values different from those of the village.

Secret lives and relationships also develop in the town. Micaela and the northerner Damián have a secret affair. After Micaela experiences life in Mexico City, she cannot accept the strict social mores of the town and becomes something of a flirt. The final result of the affair and Micaela's flirtatious ways is that Damián murders Micaela and his own father. Another relationship develops between the widow Victoria and the church bell ringer, Gabriel, who is also the town's artist and creative force, a quality that leads Victoria into this nearly disastrous affair. At the end of the novel, a young woman named María, niece of Don Dionisio, rejects her upbringing and the town's values by running away with the revolutionaries who sweep through the region.

For one scholar, *The Edge of the Storm* is not a historical novel but an intense literary study of the human patterns that make up the contradictory personality of the village.[3] Some critics have censured Yáñez for the ponderous and static quality of the first half of the novel. Joseph Sommers, however, argues that these critics have neglected the basic human drama unfolding beneath the surface.[4] He concludes astutely that the work's "ambivalence" and "universal interest" are the novel's most special qualities.[5]

*The Edge of the Storm* contains 16 chapters that unfold into a pattern of two parts. The first part consists of 7 chapters, the first of which is the "Acto preparatorio." In this chapter, which offers a static vision of life in the town, Yáñez employs few verbs—including many sentences with no verbs at all—to create a sense of virtual timelessness. The minimal sense of the movement of time operates in contrast to the forces of repression and reaction against change. Stylistic suggestions of the opposition between change and repression of change set up, in effect, the entire first part of the novel's structure, consisting of the next 6 chapters.

Yáñez did not have quite as profound an interest in oral culture as Asturias, but traces of oral culture are evident in this first part of the novel. In this context, a chapter titled "El viejo Lucas Macías" stands out. The old man Lucas Macías, the repository of oral culture in the town, remembers and relates the town's past and its traditions—the traditional role of the storyteller in oral cultures.

The eighth of the 16 chapters, "Canicas," functions as a type of intermezzo, recapitulating some of the novel's themes and prefiguring the revolution.[6] This chapter sets up the upcoming change in the town, which will now be part of the larger scene in Mexico. The chapter also introduces Gabriel, the bell ringer whose music is central to the entire town's rhythm of life. The narrator associates Gabriel's creative force with the revolution.

In the novel's second part, the ninth chapter, entitled "Gabriel and Victoria," functions as an overture to the novel's second half, and thus has a function parallel to the "Acto preparatorio," in the first half.[7] It relates the relationship of Gabriel and the attractive Victoria but it also becomes something of an abstraction.

The novel's last 7 chapters function as a mirror image of the first part, creating a symmetrical structure. They continue to portray relationships among the people in the town, as well as the growing rebellion. By the end, the hermeticism of the town is broken by the revolution.

The Catholic Church is an overwhelming presence, affecting all aspects of life and thought in the town. In its totality, however, the novel is less about religion than tyranny, as Brushwood points out: "Yáñez's novel is not antichurch or even anticlerical, as some have wished to make it; it is very much anti the tyrannies men allow themselves to create and then suffer."[8]

Rarely does one encounter a modernist novel with such a seemingly perfect harmony between form and content as *The Edge of the Storm*; it is a technical masterpiece of modernist fiction in Mexico. The two-part structure leads the reader through a process from fragmentation to harmony; the content of the novel also points to the fragmentation of the characters in the first half and their harmonious fulfillment of desires when they join the revolution. Yáñez also uses a subtle technique similar to *style indirect libre*, in which the narration moves subtly from third to first person, from omniscience to a type of interior monologue; similarly, exterior and interior forces are the thematic core of the novel. In much of the third-person narration, the narrator uses the language of the townsfolk.

In his second novel, *La creación*, Yáñez also takes great care with its form, particularly its structure. This novel deals with Gabriel Martínez, the bell ringer and creative artist from *The Edge of the Storm*, after the revolution; Gabriel also provides Yáñez with the opportunity to offer opinions about art in Mexico after the revolution. In this vein, the names of many Mexican and foreign artists appear. Gabriel is a musician and composer, and the novel relates the details of the creative process. Gabriel's career depends on two women, Victoria and María, also from *The Edge of the Storm*. Victoria is characterized as the ideal woman who functions more as an imagined than real presence for Gabriel. His relationship with her interferes with his ability to relate to empirical reality. In contrast, María operates in the real world and has the power to contribute to Gabriel's success as an artist. The idealistic composer, however, is unwilling to accept her assistance. He believes in absolute freedom of expression, the principal theme of the novel.

The structure of *La creación* reveals a relationship of theme and technique as well conceived as that in *The Edge of the Storm*. The central theme of the work is musical creation, and the formal structure of the work is divided into a four-part concerto. The first part, "Primer movimiento, *andante*," culminates in a chapter titled "coda." The remaining three parts are titled "Segundo movimiento: *creciente*," "Tercer movimiento: *galopante*," and "Cuarto movimiento: *vehemente*," each of which contains four chapters. With this structure, Yáñez tried to translate the ideal musical work to the written page.

Unfortunately, the written word is not the ideal medium to communicate musical themes. *La creación* tends to be a somewhat tedious novel, since the "action" of the work consists of the successes and failures of the creative process. In addition, much of the book reads more like an essay than a novel. One critic describes the novel's problems as follows: "Although his excellent control of language takes him as close as anyone could get, both the author and the reader stay outside the artist and talk about the process rather than experience it."[9] The reader's experience—namely, the reader's lack of direct contact with the music—is what distinguishes this well-written novel from the more successful creation of experience in *The Edge of the Storm*.

*Ojerosa y pintada* is very different in approach and content from *The Edge of the Storm* and *La creación*. Subtitled "La vida en la Ciudad de México" ("Life in Mexico City"), *Ojerosa y pintada* deals with life in the capital during a 24-hour period as seen through the eyes of a taxi driver. The novel opens dramatically with the taxi driver rushing a pregnant woman to a hospital. After that and throughout the novel, he transports individuals representing the gamut of Mexican society—a conventional middle-class family, students, intellectuals, musicians, a youth from Guerrero, businessmen, prostitutes, and a poor boy who convinces the driver to give him a free ride. Yáñez portrays unique characters, too, such as an Indian who claims to be Jesus Christ and a musician who plays the role of the creative artist, the alter ego of Gabriel in *The Edge of the Storm* and *La creación*.

*Ojerosa y pintada* seems relatively traditional and simple in technique. An omniscient narrator controls most of the narration and the novel moves from one scene to another in a systematic and clear fashion. For the most part, the characters appear only once, but the narrator describes these characters in minute detail. As José Luis Martínez points out, all of Yáñez's novels are circular in structure, and *Ojerosa y pintada* begins with a birth and ends with a death.[10]

A more precise consideration of the novel's structure reveals an organization similar to that of *The Edge of the Storm*; *Ojerosa y pintada* is developed in three parts. In the first, "Cuesta arriba," such memorable characters as the boy named Peralvillo and General Robles appear. In it, the taxi driver sees everything in a personal, intimate fashion.[11] He looks at people in terms of their private life. The second part, "Parteaguas," functions as an interlude, containing a character who is a philosopher. In the third part, "Cuesta abajo," the taxi driver is less personal in his observations.

Although not one of the major modernist novels of Yáñez or of this period, *Ojerosa y pintada* was an important contribution to the urbanization of the Mexican novel and the Latin American novel in general. Fuentes's *Where the Air is Clear* (1958) was an even more significant novel dealing with Mexico City, and these two novels (along with Luis Spota's *Casi el paraíso*) lead Mexican fiction of the 1960s away from its traditional rural settings and into new urban spaces.

In *La tierra pródiga*, Yáñez returns to a rural setting and his native state of Jalisco, but the locale is now the jungle of the Pacific Coast. The protagonist, Ricardo Guerra Victoria, is an energetic and ambitious leader in the style of the traditional Latin American *cacique*. He dominates great tracts of land and many people in the region. He wins the heart of Elena, a beautiful young woman from a local village, and carries out numerous tasks for people in the region to realize his ambitions. As his fame spreads, he becomes known by the nickname of El Amarillo.

Once he establishes his control of the region, El Amarillo exploits the land and the people mercilessly. He builds an enormous airport before bothering to construct a highway or hotel for tourists. His projects include a church that is far more luxurious and much larger than the local people need. He also exploits women, taking numerous lovers and eventually abandoning Elena. In the end, government reaction against El Amarillo causes his downfall.

Several critics have pointed out parallels between the characterization of this *cacique* and the Spanish *conquistadores* of the sixteenth century.[12] Yáñez himself has spoken of this historical referent: "underneath the surface is an historical theme of the Conquest and the times of the *conquistadores*, of the men that went off to conquer the coasts of Mexico."[13]

*La tierra pródiga* is another of Yáñez's well-structured works, this one divided into nine parts, each of which carries a title. Each of these, in turn, contains two to seven brief chapters. The first chapter, "Rueda de fieras," opens with a conversation among four local *caciques* who work for El Amarillo as they plan their strategy with the government. One of them, Medellín, serves as the contact with the government and the promoter of projects that benefit the *caciques*. In this and the following chapters, Yáñez portrays individuals in detail, revealing their character through lengthy descriptions and lively dialogue.

Although not as technically complex as *The Edge of the Storm*, *La tierra pródiga* does contain one notable technical device. Yáñez intercalates lengthy fragments of narrative in parentheses; these fragments are interior monologues that provide the novel's interiorizations. Yáñez always finds a method for revealing a deeper reality in his novels, and in this one the interior monologues are the prime method. The present circumstances in the novel are also revealed by the constant alternation between the past and the present.

Change and progress are frequently problematic concepts in Yáñez's work, and this is the case in *La tierra pródiga*. The destruction of the jungle is questioned, and the figure who dominates the land, El Amarillo, loses control at the end.

A *cacique* and patriarch also is the central character of *The Lean Lands*. The phrase *tierras flacas* of the original Spanish title (*Las tierras flacas*) does not translate well into English, but it refers to a sparse, unproductive land on which the inhabitants can barely subsist. The *cacique* is Don Epifanio Trujillo, who dominates in the region (Jalisco in the early 1920s) and begets children throughout the area. The novel has a biblical tone that is reinforced by the names of the local ranches, which are also the titles of the novel's five parts: "Betanía: la tierra o la máquina," "Jerusalén: el regreso de Miguel Arcángel," "Belén: lugar de abominación," "Babel: el día del juicio," "Damasco y Galilea: entrada de la electricidad." Other small ranches and villages have biblical names, too, as the inhabitants attempt to duplicate biblical life.

*The Lean Lands* is the story of Don Epifanio's physical deterioration and downfall. His abuses and tyrannical methods create hostilities among the local families. As a direct descendent of the Spanish *conquistadores,* Don Epifanio is seen by the townsfolk as the embodiment of political, economic, and religious authority. Eventually, he is confronted by a son, Miguel Arcángel, who represents change and progress. In fact, the confrontation between the two is portrayed symbolically as a conflict between progress and technology on the one hand, and the old agrarian society on the other. To antagonize his father, Miguel marries Florencia Sánchez and changes his name to Jacobo Gallo, thus rejecting his father's last name. Don Epifanio was expecting Miguel Arcángel to perpetuate the family name and continue ruling in the style of the patriarch. Instead, Miguel rejects his father, goes to Mexico City, and assumes a position in the bureaucracy. Later, he returns to the region as a representative of the central government to confront the Trujillo clan. As a representative of the government of General Alvaro Obregón (1920–1924), he works to integrate the region into the national economy, as well as to modernize the villages with electricity and other forms of technology.

The structure of *The Lean Lands* once again reveals a precise and harmonious organizational structure. A certain organizational rhythm is created because each of the novel's first four parts (*estancias*) contains three subdivisions (or chapters), while the fifth part contains four subdivisions. Each subdivision begins with the words of that part's title, and these beginnings always contain some folkloric content.[14] Each *estancia* also has a specific function in the development of the novel. The first establishes the situation and introduces the unforgettable characters. In the second part, Jacobo Gallo returns. The third *estancia* operates as a transitional part of the binary structure of the novel, thus having a function similar to the "Canicas" chapter in *The Edge of the Storm*.

Yáñez also integrates oral culture, as he does in *The Edge of the Storm*. Oral cultures depend heavily on the use of proverbs, and Yáñez uses proverbs repetitively throughout the novel. They create a sense of timelessness and help the reader move from one generation to the next. Transmitting knowledge from one generation to the next, of course, is one of the main functions of proverbs in oral cultures. Yáñez skillfully synthesizes oral culture and Christian tradition in this novel; both are deeply ingrained in the peasants as well as the patriarchs of *The Lean Lands*.

In conclusion, Agustín Yáñez was a major contributor to the rise of modernist fiction in Latin America during the 1940s and 1950s. Yáñez was a master of the narrative techniques associated with the aesthetics of modernism, particularly techniques of interiorization that are so effective in *The Edge of the Storm*, *La creación*, and *La tierra pródiga*. In all his novels, he constructs complex narrative structures that facilitate the penetration of deeper realities. These structures also create harmonies in his novels that initially seem chaotic.

The net effect of Yáñez's fiction is the creation of an ample panorama of a traditional and deeply Catholic society in rural Jalisco. In this society, change, progress, and modernization are ambiguous concepts. For most of the inhabitants of these novels—the peasants of rural Jalisco—change is a threat to the traditions of their society and of their church. Progress is generally seen as an unwelcome foreign phenomenon. On the other hand, these same characters frequently suffer anguished and even tortured lives within the strict boundaries of traditional society and church. Consequently, there is always a minority of characters who embrace progress and change as an escape from their dismal and limited circumstance.

Yáñez, like Asturias, was fully aware of the rich possibilities available in integrating oral culture with the novel form. For Asturias, the expression of oral culture was a special window to Indian culture. For Yáñez, oral culture expressed the mindset of descendants of both Spaniards and Indians who had not changed their ways of thinking for centuries. The proverbs and sayings of this rural Mexican oral culture represent a unique but tight synthesis of traditional Catholic and traditional agrarian cultures.

Like most modernist novelists, Yáñez wrote with the assumption that individual consciousness was central to both the creation and the reading of novels. His gift for characterizing the numerous individuals who populate his novels—always suggesting or revealing a deeper level of reality beyond their actions—is one of the major accomplishments of this pioneer modernist in Mexico.

# 4

# *The Novels of Alejo Carpentier*

Alejo Carpentier has been described as the dean of Cuban novelists and he is, indeed, the country's major novelist of the twentieth century.[1] Although belonging to the generation of Asturias and Yáñez, Carpentier had published more essays and fiction than either of these writers by the time he appeared with them on the Latin American literary scene in the 1940s. Publishing *The Kingdom of This World* in 1949, Carpentier played a major role in the reaffirmation of the right of invention. He wrote nine novels, a considerable amount of short fiction, and numerous essays—a body of work that has made him one of the century's most renowned practitioners of modernist aesthetics in Latin America. Indeed, Carpentier, along with Neruda and Borges, is a key figure in the literary tradition of which he is one of the founders.[2] Carpentier's main interests were history and time, but like the other novelists of his generation, he also was well aware of the presence of oral culture in Latin America, and traces of orality are discernible in his fiction.

Like Asturias, Carpentier was in Paris in the 1920s and in contact with the European writers of the avant-garde, principally the surrealists. He already knew French language and culture well, having studied at a high school in Paris from 1912 to 1921. After spending the next seven years in Cuba, he went into self-imposed exile to Europe in 1928. Before leaving Cuba, he served 40 days in jail for participating in political activity against the dictatorship of Gerardo Machado and he had also belonged to a group of radicals that published the magazine *Revista de Avance*. In Europe in the 1930s, he was deeply involved in an Afro-Cuban cultural and literary movement.[3] In 1939, Carpentier returned to Havana after spending 11 years in Paris, with visits to Madrid and Berlin in the 1930s.

Before the appearance of *The Kingdom of This World*, Carpentier had published the novel *Ecue-Yamba-0!* (Ecue-Yamba-O, 1933), the novella *Journey Back to the Source* (1944), and the essay *La música en*

*Cuba* (Music in Cuba, 1946). In the latter part of his career, Carpentier disavowed *Ecue-Yamba-O!*, considering it part of an immature past that he preferred forgetting. Nevertheless, this book occupies a significant place in the development of the twentieth-century Spanish American novel.[4] *Ecue-Yamba-O!* (which means "Lord, praised be thou" in an African dialect spoken in Cuba) deals with African culture in Cuba and the search for cultural identity. The novel's three parts—"Childhood," "Adolescence," and "The City"—follow the life of the black protagonist, Menegildo Cué. Carpentier's use of short chapters and repetitions of chapter titles was an effective narrative strategy in this first novel.

After a hiatus of well over a decade, Carpentier began his second and recognized career as a novelist with *The Kingdom of This World*, a brief four-part novel set in Haiti during its early independence at the beginning of the nineteenth century. The novel relates the life of a character named Ti Noel as he develops in each of the book's four parts. The first part, which consists of seven brief chapters, narrates a rebellion under the leadership of a man named MacKandal. The second, which takes place 20 years later, also contains seven chapters and tells of the historic Bouckman massacre and of a yellow fever epidemic. The seven-chapter third part deals with the rule of Henri Christophe, and the fourth part relates the coming of the mulattos.

Carpentier's prologue to this novel provides some of the historical context to the work; he explains that in 1943 he visited the ruins of Sans-Souci in Haiti that had been the property of Henri Christophe. He points out that during his stay in Haiti he was in daily contact with "algo que podríamos llamar lo real maravilloso" ["something that we could call the marvelous real"].[5] He found the country to be a land of miracles, prodigious acts, incredible events. He ends the prologue by asking "¿pero qué es la historia de América toda sino una crónica de lo real-maravilloso?" ["but what is the history of all the Americas but a chronicle of the marvelous real?"].[6] This affirmation about "the marvelous real" became a basic tenet of Carpentier's interpretation of Latin American reality, as well as a foundation for the Latin American concept of "magic realism."[7]

However, the most appropriate description of *The Kingdom of This World*, as Roberto González Echevarría has pointed out, is that of fantastic literature.[8] Carpentier searches for the marvelous beneath the surface of Latin American consciousness.[9] Since the marvelous reveals itself to those who believe it, Carpentier's concept of the marvelous is basically a matter of faith.

An omniscient and detached narrator relates *The Kingdom of This World* with a distance that creates an illusion of objectivity. Given this objective tone, the prologue's explanation of the novel's historical veracity, and its historical characters, *The Kingdom of This World* can be read as an historical account. The only deviation from this interpretation is the narrator's relating, in a matter-of-fact way, of the transformation of certain characters into nonhuman forms. In these passages, Carpentier appropriates oral-culture forms; such transformations are typical of oral storytelling.[10]

*The Kingdom of This World* does not offer the technical virtuosity of the flashy Asturias in *El Señor Presidente* or the equally ambitious Yáñez in *The Edge of the Storm*. Carpentier's idea of innovation did not include the manipulation of fragmented structures or multiple points of view. His method for reaching a deeper layer beneath the surface of reality was not the employment of modernist strategies, but oral-storytelling techniques. As Carpentier understood the right of invention in the 1940s, the Latin American writer's special task was to express "the marvelous real." One innovation was freely incorporating oral-cultural traditions in stories that included human transformations.

With *The Lost Steps*, a characteristic writing style of Carpentier becomes more apparent: baroque language, lengthy and detailed descriptive passages, and minute descriptions of architecture. Written in the form of a diary, *The Lost Steps* is a first-person narration with "a greater sense of intimacy" than is common in Carpentier's fiction.[11] The narrator-protagonist takes a journey through time into a jungle, going back to the origins of human culture or creation. At the same time, it is a trip back to preliterate society and oral culture.

The protagonist of *The Lost Steps* is a musician whose career and life are in crisis. He is increasingly aware that his creative ability is being affected by the commercial demands to which he must respond in order to earn a living. His relationships with women are as unfulfilling as his career. His wife, Ruth, is an actress and unsatisfactory as a mate. His lover, Mouche, is an astrologer who seems as vapid as her career. He finds an opportunity for possible fulfillment: a friend offers the opportunity to organize an expedition to search for primitive instruments that might explain the origin of music. He accepts the invitation and departs with Mouche.

The couple makes their trip into the interior of an unnamed Latin American country (which the reader can surmise is Venezuela). As they move inland, they leave behind more and more elements associated with Western civilized society. At the same time, the protagonist's interest in finding the musical instruments grows and he becomes increasingly rejuvenated. Mouche, on the other hand, grows progressively older and irrelevant in this natural environment. Eventually, after she is confronted by a woman named Rosario, who is associated with the telluric forces of the jungle, and she soon returns to the city. Rosario then becomes the protagonist's companion. They eventually come upon a massive rock formation that rises above the jungle. They seem to have arrived at the beginning of time or Genesis, a world inhabited by the primitive society of the original creation.

Realizing that he does not fit into this primitive society and needing paper in order to create, the protagonist decides to return to the city. There, he finds himself even more distanced from Ruth and wanting to return to the jungle. Once he begins his return trip he realizes that he does not fit into modern urban society and that his role as a creative artist is to mediate between contemporary and prehistoric times.

*The Lost Steps* allows its reader to consider different types of disorder and formlessness.[12] Modern society seems to be on the edge of dissolution. In his journey into the past, as Raymond Souza points out, "the protagonist encounters a reality that is in the process of forming, where vital forces have not yet imposed order on existence."[13] This disorder is the chaos that precedes the creation of new forms.

Roberto González Echevarría reads *The Lost Steps* as a break from the Spenglerian ideological framework of Carpentier's earlier work.[14] In this novel, Carpentier writes with a different and conflicting conception of humanity and history: Sartrean existentialism.[15] González Echevarría states: "Sartrean concepts like 'authenticity' to mention only one, surface in this novel, and the predicament of the protagonist, caught between a search for his essence in the past and a commitment to the present-in-history, is clearly Sartrean."[16] González Echevarría also points to Carpentier's desire to write the total novel: "the novel shows a totalizing desire on both the level of personal and world history. . . ."[17]

*The Lost Steps* is best understood as the story of a writing-culture intellectual who makes a journey into the orality of the past. Ong has pointed out that once preliterate orality is lost to writing, there is often a nostalgic sense of loss.[18] Once the protagonist arrives in the jungle, he speaks nostalgically of "un encanto que habían perdido" ["a charm that they had lost"].[19] Passages of the novel that have been described as examples of magic realism relate stories of incredible events in the natural world of the jungle. Ong points out, however, that oral cultures tend to relate natural events as part of the human lifeworld. Consequently, stories such as that of the Gusano [Worm], which is apparently responsible for a series of inexplicable acts in chapter 7, might be called magic realism by some readers; stories such as these are typical of oral cultures.

Several other factors suggest that the protagonist's journey is a return to an oral culture. Oral cultures tend to exist in a continual present[20]; the protagonist remarks that he is surprised how Rosario lives so much in the present, without thinking about the past or the future (chap. 23). Later, seemingly sensing the tension between writing and oral language, the protagonist questions what his real language is (chap. 30).

With the novella El acoso (The pursuit), Carpentier continues his fictionalization of issues related to time: the structure of the novella has parallels with Beethoven's Third Symphony and the text is supposed to take 46 minutes to read—the same amount of time that it takes to play Beethoven's symphony. Multiple narrators relate the stories of a political activist and a ticket seller through a series of recollections of these two parallel yet separate consciousnesses. At the end of the novella, the protagonist, who is a fugitive from authorities, is thrown out of the church where he has sought sanctuary.

In El acoso the reader finds Carpentier the modernist experimenting with narrative technique as he had in no other work. Unlike Carpentier's previous texts, however, the novella contains none of the fantastic elements associated with magic realism or oral cultures. The main theme of El acoso is the artist in contemporary society, and the artist's alienation is expressed in terms of a desire for the absolute.[21]

Carpentier published a volume of four stories in Spanish entitled Guerra del tiempo (War of time) in 1958, including El acoso and the novella Viaje a la semilla (the latter of which had originally appeared in Spanish in 1944). The two other stories were "El camino de Santiago" (The road to Santiago) and "Semejante a la noche" (Similar to the night). "El camino de Santiago" is a story set in the sixteenth century. A Spanish soldier named Juan de Ambaceres attempts to travel to Santiago de Compostela to confess his sins, but becomes distracted by alcohol and ends up in Sevilla, where he catches a ship to the Americas, landing in Havana. After having killed a man during one of his drunken episodes, he flees back to Spain. Once there, he becomes a storyteller of the marvels of the Americas. At the end, he and his collaborators prepare for yet another trip to the Americas. The story is much more complex than this summary would suggest, for it contains, in fact, four "Juan" figures. The story suggests that history repeats itself and human beings change, but that the events of history remain essentially the same.[22]

"Semejante a la noche" is the shortest story in the volume and another of Carpentier's modernist experiments with narrative technique. It deals with six historical moments.[23] The protagonist of the first of these is an ancient Greek warrior who plans to save Helen of Troy. He then is transformed into a sixteenth-century Spanish conquistador embarking on a trip to exploit the riches of the New World. The third protagonist is a French colonizer on his way to North America in the seventeenth century, while the fourth historical setting occurs during the Middle Ages and the Crusades. The next historical moment is World War II, and the protagonist is an American soldier readying himself to invade Normandy. The last scene returns the reader to the Homeric period, where the demoralized warrior observes how much better off the officers are than he. "Semejante a la noche" contains three themes that are common in Carpentier's work: the decadence of the West, revolution, and the immutability of human beings throughout history.[24]

*Explosion in a Cathedral* deals with the ideas of the French Revolution as they spread throughout the Caribbean between 1790 and 1809.[25] The novel's main character, Victor Hugues, is an historical figure who governed the island of Guadeloupe during the French Revolution. The novel begins in Cuba in 1790; a character named Carlos discovers that his father has died and left the family estate to him, his sister, and a cousin, Esteban. With no parental authority or direction, their lives become both carefree and disordered. Victor arrives on the scene and gives their lives some direction by influencing them with the ideas he holds as a Freemason. Esteban eventually goes to Europe with Victor, and they both participate in the French Revolution. They return to Guadeloupe to carry out the revolution, and Esteban is "emotionally persecuted on the paradoxes of the revolutionary process."[26] He feels that the ideas he had learned from the French Revolution are being debased by political maneuvering; Esteban thinks that Victor trades power for political ideas far too readily. Eventually, Victor's cold political opportunism, contradictions, and lack of empathy for the very people whom he supposedly supports result in his failure in Guadeloupe. Nevertheless, he obtains an appointment to govern Cayenne, where he clings to power. Esteban returns to Cuba, where he meets with a woman named Sofía, who eventually flees to be with Victor. Esteban is imprisoned in Cuba for protecting Sofía's revolutionary activity. He remains faithful to revolutionary ideals to the end.

As in several of Carpentier's earlier works, the forces of history dominate over the will of individuals. Souza points out, appropriately, that "instinct overcomes rational judgment as individuals are swept by the forces of history."[27] Even though the ideas and political ideals that individuals may hold are their own, in Carpentier's fiction in general and in *Explosion in a Cathedral* specifically, these are really ideas of the times.

With *Explosion in a Cathedral*, Carpentier has achieved a mastery of language and style that are the mark of a true master of the craft of fiction. In this novel, Carpentier writes with great elegance and polish, taking the reader deeply into the eighteenth and nineteenth centuries with his profound and detailed knowledge of these periods.

*Concierto barroco* (Baroque concert) is a short novel that is far less ambitious than *Explosion in a Cathedral*. Carpentier continues his attack on Western concepts of time, beginning his novel in the eighteenth century in Latin America and ending in twentieth-century Europe. At the end, the black Cuban slave Filomeno leaves his master to attend a Louis Armstrong concert in Paris. This novel represents a return to the Afro-Antillian movement, since the protagonist is black. In it, Carpentier rewrites the colonial poem *El enigma de los esterlines* by Silvestre de Balboa y Troya de Quesada,[28] considered by many scholars to be "the first poem written in Cuba."[29] Carpentier's Filomeno is the descendent of Salvador, a black man in the poem. The major scene in *Concierto barroco*, an enormous jam session in the Ospedale della Pietá, echoes a celebration at the end of the *Espejo de paciencia*, when the inhabitants of Bayamo celebrate the bishop's rescue.[30]

In 1974, the same year that *Concierto barroco* appeared, Carpentier published *Reasons of State*, a novel about a dictator (several Latin American writers wrote novels dealing with dictators in the 1970s[31]).

Carpentier's dictator is a synthesis of several historical figures from Latin America, the most important being Cuba's Gerardo Machado. In his attempt to appear refined, the dictator spends half of his life in Europe. He is a tragicomic figure, and *Reasons of State* is Carpentier's only comic novel.

His last two novels, *La consagración de la primavera* (The consecration of the spring, 1979) and *El arpa y la sombra* (The harp and the shadow, 1979), are two short autobiographical works. In *La consagración de la primavera*, he creates three autobiographical characters—an architect, a writer, and a musician. This historical novel begins with the Spanish Civil War and ends with the Cuban Revolution. Written while Carpentier knew he was dying of cancer, *El arpa y la sombra* depicts Carpentier as Christopher Columbus. It deals with the investigation that was carried out in the nineteenth century surrounding the Vatican's consideration of Columbus for canonization. Columbus is not canonized, a decision that perhaps Carpentier relates to the fact that he was considered for the Nobel Prize but never received it.[32]

In conclusion, Carpentier was a major practitioner of modernist aesthetics for several decades, and his novels of the 1940s and 1950s were important contributions to the reaffirmation of the Latin American writers' right of invention. In his early fiction, such as *The Kingdom of This World* and *The Lost Steps,* one important method for expressing this right was "the marvelous real." For Carpentier, this marvelous quality of Latin American reality was what differentiated Latin American culture from European culture. Carpentier was fully aware of the presence of oral culture in Latin America; his early novels contained passages based on an oral culture, even though he exploited this facet of Latin American reality far less than did Asturias and Yáñez.

In this generation of Latin American modernists, however, Carpentier was one of the most accomplished stylists, even when compared to other masterful craftsmen. As one critic of Cuban literature has affirmed in a statement about Carpentier's novels, "his language is elegant, polished, and a testimony of his knowledge."[33] Carpentier's nine novels are, indeed, testimony to his maturity in the exercise of the right of invention and represent his vast knowledge of the history and cultures of Latin America.

# 5

# *The Novels of Leopoldo Marechal and Juan Carlos Onetti*

Modernist aesthetics arrived relatively early and with major impact in the River Plate region. The pioneer figure in promoting these new literary aesthetics in Buenos Aires, of course, was Borges. The rise of the modernist novel in South America's Southern Cone region, however, was spearheaded by the Argentine Leopoldo Marechal and the Uruguayan Juan Carlos Onetti. Marechal wrote the seminal novel *Adán Buenosayres* (Adam Buenosayres, 1948) and two other brief and far less significant fictions; Onetti wrote over a dozen novels of consistently high quality. Both were urban and urbane writers whose interests lay far from Carpentier's "marvelous real," Latin American magic realism, or the oral cultures of the Andean and Caribbean regions.

Marechal was not only a novelist but also a recognized playwright, essayist, and poet; he published several volumes of poetry from the 1920s to the 1940s. Like Asturias, Yáñez, and Carpentier, he was interested in European avant-garde writing. Marechal's involvement with the avant-garde took the form of his participation in the cultural activities of the Martin Fierro group in Buenos Aires in the 1920s.[1]

Onetti was a highly productive fiction writer who also published a few essays. A native of Montevideo, he first gained recognition as a writer in Uruguay's capital in the late 1930s. In 1939, Onetti was involved in founding the weekly cultural magazine *Marcha*, an organ that has been seminal in Uruguay and influential throughout Latin America. He worked as a journalist and editor during much of his writing career, which had been relatively ignored until late in his life, when some of his novels were translated into English.

# Leopoldo Marechal's *Adán Buenosayres*

Marechal's reputation as a novelist, as well as his contribution to the rise of the modernist novel in Latin America and to the reaffirmation of the right of invention during the 1940s and 1950s, rests entirely on *Adán Buenosayres*. Lengthy, complex, and sometimes daunting, this novel had its genesis in Paris in the 1930s, when, according to Marechal, he was suffering a "profound" spiritual crisis and wrote a first draft.

*Adán Buenosayres* consists of seven *libros* (books) that are divided into three parts. The first part, which contains five of these books (368 pages), deals with the character named Adán Buenosayres as well as his cohorts. The second part, book six (36 pages), is Adán Buenosayres's "*Cuaderno de tapas azules*" ("Notebook with blue covers"). The third part, book seven (239 pages), is entitled "*Viaje a la oscura ciudad de Cacodelphia*" ("Trip to the dark city of Cacodelphia").

In the first five books, the reader observes Adán Buenosayres in a lengthy dialogue with his friends, most of whom are intellectuals and writers. In the "Prólogo indispensable" preceding the five books, the narrator tells of the burial of Adán Buenosayres, an act that is described not as the death of a man but as the material of a "poema concluido." The narrator-author then explains that Adán had given him two manuscripts on his deathbed: the *Cuaderno de tapas azules* and the *Viaje a la oscura ciudad de Cacodelphia*. After reviewing them and deciding that they merited publication as valuable contributions to Argentine letters, the narrator-author decides to provide a portrait of the author and protagonist of these two pieces. After further consideration, however, he decides to portray the protagonist in the context of the conflicts and crises in his own life. The result is the five books that follow the prologue, covering one day in the life of Adán Buenosayres. The narrator-author then sets the tone for the novel by mentioning that he himself wrote the first draft for this work in Paris in 1930 and then suffered a spiritual crisis. At the end, he debunks certain traditional literary concepts, such as the idea of "originality" and the cliché that any similarity between the characters and real people is coincidental.

The first book, which begins on the 28th of April sometime in the 1920s, tells of Adán Buenosayres's life in Buenos Aires as a poet and intellectual fascinated with Roman and Greek literature. It also tells of his idealized love for Solveig Admussen, and how he suffers for her as well as from a general existential anguish. The narrator occasionally intervenes directly to make comments to the reader about the characters or the novel itself. There is mention of the *Cuaderno de tapas azules*, Adán's prized work that he gives to Solveig. In this chapter, the narrator also introduces Samuel Tesler, a Russian emigré from Odessa who practices philosophy.

The second, third, fourth, and fifth books continue with the story of Adán, his love for Solveig, and his intellectual friends. Adán's walks around Buenos Aires are portrayed in the epic terms of the hero on a journey. He participates in a lengthy literary *tertulia* with his friends—a *soirée* where they discuss Argentine and world literature, particularly the former. They enter into heated debate over the relative value of traditional Buenos Aires versus modern Buenos Aires. Adán tends to be more of an observer than participant in the discussion, which sometimes involves esoteric knowledge, such as references to the Zohar. At another level, the text functions as a roman á clef that satirizes certain Argentine intellectual figures of the 1920s, who also criticize and satirize Argentine society of the time, particularly its new bourgeois values.

The sixth book (and the second part of the novel), "*Cuaderno de tapas azules*," is Adán's notebook in which he has recorded the history of his soul and his emotional states since childhood. To some extent, it is also a history of his insanity. He probes into the depths of his afflicted soul, letting his imagination run free, and reveals his dreams. At the end of this tortuous spiritual journey, he concludes his notebook by observing that his life finally has a sure direction and hope.

The seventh book (and third part of the novel) is Adán's surreal trip through the nine levels or circles of the dark city of Cacodelphia (a name that plays with the word for excrement in Spanish). The astrologer Schultze serves as Adán's guide, explaining in the beginning that Cacodelphia is not a mythological city but a real one. After approaching a foggy part of town, they descend into its center. (The reader is warned early in the book either to return to Buenos Aires or to continue the trip.) During the playful and satirical journey, Marechal continues his critique of Argentine literature and society. Numerous classical allusions throughout the novel also make it a parody of classical texts such as *The Odyssey*. As they travel through the nine spirals, the city is obviously quite similar to Buenos Aires in the 1920s, but also with many traditional images of hell.

In the 1940s, *Adán Buenosayres* received relatively little attention. It was virtually unknown outside Argentina, and Marechal's affiliation with Perón probably contributed to the novel's cool reception in 1948. Since the 1960s, however, there has been something of a Marechal revival in Argentina; writers of several generations have expressed their admiration for his writings.

Brushwood reads *Adán Buenosayres* as an important satirical novel dealing with the world of avant-garde literati in Buenos Aires in the 1920s.[2] An intellectually induced circumstance created by the personalities in the novel is the basis for the work's style. For Lindstrom, Adán is a metaphor and can be seen as a "figure of man at the outset of life, or a representative of the human quest, and he incarnates the Argentine, the man of Buenos Aires, or the city itself figured in human form."[3] Adán, however, alternates between metaphorical and realistic traits, just as the novel alternates between an abstract and realistic mode of representation. The novel's themes follow a similar dual pattern, dealing with the reality of Buenos Aires as well as philosophical concerns, both neo-Platonic and Christian.

The humorous effects and remarkable style in *Adán Buenosayres* depend, to a large extent, on Marechal's uses of language. The text's standard discourse is an elegant literary style into which Marechal inserts colloquial or vulgar words and phrases, thereby creating a farcical effect. The vulgar language tends to emphasize the anal, and the humorous consequences tend to deflate the pretentious.[4]

Another noteworthy narrative technique that Marechal uses is a special narrator. The primary narrator throughout the novel is third-person omniscient, but the narrator often communicates the language and perceptions of Adán himself. In some fragments of the novel, the narration moves to a second person, with Adán's voice speaking to himself. In a few cases, a voice from the past speaks to a self in the present.

# The Novels of Juan Carlos Onetti

Onetti published fiction from the 1930s to the 1970s, but his most important novels appeared in the 1940s, 1950s, and early 1960s. His most lasting contributions to the rise of modernist fiction in Latin

America were *El pozo* (The pit, 1939), *Tierra de nadie* (No man's land, 1941), *A Brief Life* (1950), and *Los adioses* (The good byes, 1954). He wrote novels about isolated and alienated individuals who tend to lead morose and anguished lives. The backdrop for these novels is the dreary and sordid urban setting of his fictional port city Santa María. Later in his career he published *Dejemos hablar al viento* (Let's let the wind speak, 1979), and he was awarded the Miguel de Cervantes Prize in Spain in 1980.

In Onetti's first published novel, *El pozo*, there is virtually no action. It is a detailed study of the protagonist, Eladio Linacero, a writer who seems to be an alter ego of Onetti. A prototypical Onetti character, Linacero suffers from alienation and anguish. An early experiment with the world of dreams, *El pozo* is an interior monologue that deals with an interior and external world that are equally nightmarish. Linacero recalls having raped an innocent girl; he dreams of utopias despite his own moral degradation. His narrative is his attempt to capture, on his fortieth birthday, the essence of his existence. This confrontation with his life often returns to the corporal, even though he is ostensibly interested in abstraction.

In the more complex *Tierra de nadie*, a character named Diego de Aránzuru leaves his position as a lawyer in order to search for more substance and meaning in life. He is juxtaposed with a panoply of other characters, including an artist, an aspiring writer, and a taxidermist. They suffer a generalized indifference that Onetti seems to think is typical of the inhabitants of Buenos Aires. These characters engage in a variety of friendly and antagonistic relationships, meeting by chance in a multiplicity of dismal urban settings.

One of the most important features of *Tierra de nadie* is the experimental narrative technique. Onetti uses fragmentation to create a kaleidoscope effect, even though there is no one particular situation to fictionalize. Rather than heightened awareness, this technique produces an effect of chaos.[5] His use of this narrative technique was relatively early in Latin America.

With *A Brief Life* Onetti began to receive the acclaim he deserved. Considered by one informed critic as Onetti's "first consistently mature work," this novel also lays the groundwork for the Uruguayan writer's fictional world.[6] The setting in mythical Santa María seems to be an amalgam of Montevideo, Buenos Aires, and a dream world. The narrator-protagonist, Brausen, is another of Onetti's writer alter egos who suffers from isolation and alienation.

He writes fiction and screenplays, bringing fictional characters and situations into existence, a situation that provides a metafictional quality to the novel. Beyond this, the basic plot involves Brausen's imaginary and real incursions into an apartment next to his own, a space occupied by a psychologically warped and alcoholic prostitute. This and other unsavory relationships make Brausen's life an exercise in dementia and meaninglessness.

A common criticism of *A Brief Life* and other novels by Onetti is that the speech of his narrators is not differentiated from that of his characters. His narrators and his characters do indeed tend to express themselves in the same morose tone.[7] Nevertheless, *A Brief Life* offers the postmodern reader a fascinating exercise in metafictional play, indistinguishable identities, and blurred borders.

*A Brief Life* is a mature work that fictionalizes a somber world of disillusionment.[8] The complex interaction between Brausen and his fictional alter egos (Díaz Grey and Arce) makes the novel an engaging experience for the reader that few modernist texts had accomplished by the 1950s in Latin America. This interaction makes any attempt at definitive interpretation an exercise as useless and potentially meaningless as the lives of the characters.

Onetti's mature fiction and many of his obsessions continue with *Los adioses*. Although not one of his major works, this novel complements *A Brief Life* by marking Onetti's transition to an interest in metafiction. Disenchantment and a sense of futility continue in *Los adioses*, but there is a change in narrative technique. The novel deals with disenchanted individuals who live in the past, victims of tuberculosis who await their inevitable deaths in a town in the hills.

A narrator within the story creates ambiguities between fiction and reality similar to those in *A Brief Life*. This narrator is a detached figure who witnesses and presents the events to the reader from his sordid and biased point of view.[9] He is owner of a local store who witnesses everything that happens in the town. On the surface, this centrally located observer, who has seen many lives and deaths, seems to be a reliable narrator. The exceptional detail of his observations also contributes to the verisimilitude of the story. A more careful reading of the novel reveals that the apparent objectivity of the narrator is anything but objective.[10]

*Los adioses* invites the reader to reevaluate both the reading and writing processes. As in Yáñez, Marechal, and many other modernist writers, ambiguity is the key to these processes and the essence of

Onetti's success. Onetti thus represents an early case of metafictional theorization in a novel: "His theorizing in *Los adioses* deals with the problem of perspective and narrative point of view."[11]

In *Para una tumba sin nombre* (For a tomb without a name, 1959), Onetti returns to Santa María. Now the narrator-witness is Díaz Grey, who also provides the perspectives of several characters. He relates the story of a young woman, Rita, and her relationships with several individuals and her goat. Working as a prostitute, she uses her goat as a tool to solicit men on the streets of Buenos Aires. When she was younger, she had sexual encounters with Marcos Bergner, meetings which had been secretly observed by Jorge Malabia. The latter becomes obsessed with Rita and feels he has the right to possess her. Inexplicably, he uses her for prostitution, even though financial gain does not seem to be his motive. At the end, he takes her to Santa María, where she will eventually occupy a nameless tomb.

As narrator, Díaz Grey demonstrates no interest in "objectivity." Rather, he freely interjects his opinions about literary creation, including a series of "suggestions" about fiction writing. As a result, *Para una tumba sin nombre* also has metafictional qualities. These comments in the context of the total novel suggest that art is perhaps richer and more perfect than life.[12]

*The Shipyard* (1961) also functions in the mythical realm of Santa María. It deals with characters named Junta Larsen and Jeremías Petrus, but the novel's most important topics are time and space. The work's opening paragraph announces Larsen's return to Santa María, leaving the exact circumstances ambiguous. It eventually becomes evident that this deflated and defeated man is returning to the *astillero* (shipyard) in an attempt to find some meaning in life. When he had been there when he was younger, he had been more optimistic. One critic sees Larsen's return as a symbolic challenge to time: "The very idea of the undertaking is defiance, an arrogant and desperate challenge to time, since it is attempted within the very heart of its destructive emanations."[13]

The cyclical patterns in *The Shipyard* seem to offer some variation on the typical Onetti novel. Larsen's return to the shipyard and to the past is one way in which this pattern is played out. In reality, however, the basic human circumstance is the same here as it had been in all of Onetti's fiction: a return to the past brings the character to a meaningless present and a bleak future. Larsen moves forward in his search for meaning; Petrus functions as the counterpoint of death. Besides these two main characters, there are minor ones, Kunz and Gálvez, whose only possible actions are empty motions. In the end, Larsen loses his battle with time, accepts his failure in the space of the past, and accepts death. Kadir explains Larsen's situation: "He abandons precisely that which he sought to redeem. In the face of time, then, nothing human is redeemable, neither in the work of man, symbolized by the shipyard, nor his life."[14]

*The Shipyard* is narrated by a third-person narrator with a type of omniscience often limited to that of a witness in the shipyard. This narrator's limits result in certain necessary ambiguities that are the essence of Onettian technique. For example, the narrator speculates about the characters as much as he relates their qualities with omniscient certainty.

*Juntacadáveres* (The body collector, 1964) is directly connected with *The Shipyard* and is the story of Larsen's establishment of a brothel in Santa María. This is the only one of Onetti's novels in which the action takes precedence over the development of character.[15] Larsen's story and anecdotes about the brothel are more significant than any individual personality. Díaz Grey, Jorge Malabia, and Marcos Bergner appear once again, and the changes in the situation are the main interest of the novel. Once again, the protagonist attempts to find some thread of hope in a dismal world of ennui but is overwhelmed by utter cynicism.

In the latter part of his career, Onetti published two books of fiction: *La muerte y la niña* (Death and the little girl, 1973) and *Tiempo de abrazar* (Time of embrace, 1973). The latter is a volume of fiction containing part of one of the first novels that Onetti wrote and some short stories. These two works contribute nothing new to Onetti's total work. Rather, they reinforce the same themes and techniques he observed since the 1940s.

# Conclusion

In similar ways Marechal and Onetti helped to create a more modern and cosmopolitan literature in the Southern Cone in particular, and in Latin America in general. Both were atypical and unlikely candidates for one day being considered as leading modernist writers, for neither seemed, on the surface, to be sophisticated technicians of modernist narrative strategies. Nevertheless, both writers were masters of ambiguity who created very special kinds of third-person narrators. They also made some relatively early incursions into metafiction.

Marechal and Onetti saw their respective nations in difficult circumstances, which formed the basis for the spiritual or cultural crisis that many of their fictional characters suffered. Their novels, then, were spiritual and philosophical journeys for many of their characters and even for the authors. They reconfigured the very idea of what a novel could be in Latin America, often using innovative technique and demonstrating irreverent attitudes. Both writers found ways to use the traditional third-person narrator and conventional literary language in unexpected and effective ways.

# 6

# The Rise of The Brazilian Modernist Novel: Lins Do Rêgo, Amado, Ramos, and de Queiroz

A group of writers from the northeast region were the key novelists responsible for the rise of the modernist novel in Brazil. Modernist aesthetic ideas were popularized in Brazil in the 1920s with the Semana de Arte Moderna. Nevertheless, it was primarily the fiction of José Lins do Rêgo, Jorge Amado, Graciliano Ramos, and Rachel de Queiroz that modernized the novel in Brazil. Generally speaking, these writers began to exercise the right of invention along modernist lines well before the phenomenon occurred in the Spanish-speaking world, where it became more evident in the mid-1940s.

Novelists such as Miguel Angel Asturias and Agustín Yáñez had practiced a modernist type of regionalism—a transcendent regionalism of universal interest as opposed to a more traditional regionalism.[1] These four Brazilian novelists, who were born or lived in the northeastern states of Bahia, Sergipe, Alagaos, Pernambuco, Parahyba, Rio Grande do Norte, and Ceará, wrote of the arid land in this region called the *sertão*.

## José Lins do Rêgo

José Lins do Rêgo was a pioneer among the northeastern novelists and a leader in the modernization of the Brazilian novel. Unlike Marechal and Onetti, Lins do Rêgo did not engage in playful invention or existential anguish. He wrote more in the vein of Asturias and Yáñez, drawing from oral tradition and the techniques of oral storytelling. According to Mario de Andrade, one of the prominent novelists of the previous generation, Lins do Rêgo was to modern literature what Villa-Lobos was to music and what Portinari was to painting.[2]

Lins do Rêgo was born in 1901 in the agricultural zone of southern Parahyba. He was reared on a plantation of the *sertão* by his aunts and a grandfather. His early novels arc set on a sugarcane plantation similar to the one where he grew up. In the 1920s, he met the celebrated essayist and social thinker Gilberto Freyre, who had a lasting impact on Lins do Rêgo. He published several novels, becoming "the most representative of the novelists of the Northeast."[3]

He published a series of novels in the 1930s, beginning with *Doidinho* (Little boy, 1932), followed by *Menino de engenho* (Plantation lad, 1935), *O Moleque Ricardo* (Black boy Ricardo, 1936), *Fogo morto* (Dead fire, 1934), and *Usina* (Sugar refinery, 1936). Lins do Rêgo's main interests were social, and his novels generally dealt with the conflict of human beings versus the environment in the changing social patterns of the land.[4]

His early works are a cycle of novels dealing with the development of the protagonist, Carlos, from childhood to adulthood. *Doidinho* can be read as Lins do Rêgo memoir of his childhood. The novel is virtually plotless and in this sense an early version of some modernist texts. The protagonist is a child whose mentally ill father kills the boy's mother, resulting in the child being reared by his grandparents. The novel describes the impact of eight years of plantation life on the child. His behavior seems to be conditioned by his special relationships with the land and social conditions. In the end, *Doidinho* is a subtle psychological portrayal and the author's exposition about the formation of the typical Brazilian character.

In Lins do Rêgo's next novel, *Menino de engenho,* the story of Carlos continues. He attends a private high school, where he learns of religion, becomes skeptical about religion, and eventually experiences different kinds of love and sexual encounters. Carlos enjoys reading and writing, and so the novel provides a glimpse of the formation of a future writer.

In *Fogo morto,* Carlos has graduated from law school and is a young adult in his twenties. He refuses to take over his aging grandfather's plantation and finds his only refuge in life in the form of an affair with the wife of a cousin. This novel is really about the decline of the patriarchal order in northeastern Brazil. *O Moleque Ricardo* is the story of Carlos's black friend Ricardo. He suffers the loss of his wife and works in Recife, where he realizes he is worse off than he would be as a slave on the plantation. In the novels, Lins do Rêgo develops a series of parallels between life in the city and life on the plantation. His fifth novel, *Usina,* deals with inmates on a prison island. The author studies the relationship between a murderer and Ricardo. It also deals with the relationship between people and the environment in the changing society of Brazil's northeast region.

With *Eurídice* (1948), Lins do Rêgo participated in the general movement of the rise of modernist fiction in Latin America. Although the author had explored some psychological aspects of characters in his five-novel cycle, in *Eurídice,* he fully exploits the possibilities of the psychological novel, with ample interiorizations of the characters. Here, Lins do Rêgo abandoned his lifetime interest in the land of the northeast and concentrated for the first time on the human consciousness. *Eurídice* is a work of maturity in the context of both Lins do Rêgo's fiction and the modernist novel in Brazil.

Generally speaking, Lins do Rêgo is a master of storytelling whose simplicity of style and lack of concern for narrative technique do not place him in the avant-garde of the Latin American modernist movement in the 1940s. Nevertheless, his later incursions into interiorization and *Eurídice* place him clearly among the first generation of modernists in Latin America. His interest in developing universal themes in a regional setting make him one of the most prominent Latin American novelists to practice transcendent regionalism.

# Jorge Amado

Author of over two dozen novels, Jorge Amado has been one of the most prolific and internationally acclaimed Brazilian writers of the century. Initially, he was no more committed to technical innovation per se than was Lins do Rêgo, although his vast literary career, which spanned the period from the 1930s to the 1990s, has contributed significantly to the modernization of the Brazilian novel. His early fiction, published from the 1930s to the 1950s, was as overtly political as that of any of his contemporaries in Latin America; with respect to political interests and literary tendencies, his most obvious counterpart writing in Spanish was Miguel Angel Asturias. Since the publication of *Gabriela, Clove and Cinnamon* in 1958, however, he has chosen to be less explicit in his political intentions. His international popularity flourished with *Dona Flor and Her Two Husbands* (1969), which was also made into a commercially successful movie. Amado's own commercial success, as well as changes in his aesthetic and political agenda, has lead to the recent increase in critical attention given to his work among academic scholars.

Jorge Amado was born in 1912 in the northeastern region of Bahia, where his father owned a cacao plantation. In the 1920s, Amado and his intellectual friends in Bahia were enthusiasts of the modernist movement in São Paulo and were rebels against many cultural and political conventions. At the age of 18, Amado published his first novel, *O país do carnaval* (Carnival land, 1932). His other early works were *Cacao* (1933) and *Suor* (Sweat, 1934). Most critics agree that his most important of the early works was *The Violent Land* (1943). Since then, he has published over 20 novels. He has received numerous international literary prizes and by the 1970s and 1980s was recognized as one of Latin America's preeminent novelists.

*O país do carnaval*, Amado's first amateurish attempt at writing a novel, deals with Paulo Rigger, the son of a Brazilian plantation owner who grows cacao. Rigger is engaged in a search throughout the novel as he attempts to become a journalist and an intellectual. He has numerous affairs with women and becomes involved in endless conversations about everything from religion and politics to love and marriage. Neither his career, his affairs, nor his discussions, however, lead to anything of substance.

Amado wrote three novels involving cacao, the most accomplished of which was *The Violent Land*. The first was *Cacao*, a sketch of life on a cacao plantation. The second was *The Violent Land*, a work of epic grandeur. It tells the story of the conflict between cacao landowners to acquire additional land, eventually hiring private armies to help them in the fight. In the end, everyone becomes a victim of the cherished cacao land. *The Violent Land* is a psychological study of its main characters, making Amado a pioneer of the interiorized novel in Brazil. The third novel of this cycle, *São Jorge dos Ilhéus* (1944), brings the story of the landowners to a close in the 1930s.

In *Suor* and *Jubiabá*, Amado the social critic enters into issues of class differences and class conflict. *Suor* tends to be more of a sketch of various situations than a well-developed novel. *Jubiabá* was Amado's first full-length novel and it was applauded by critics for his efforts to incorporate African-Brazilian culture. Two other novels, *Seara vermelha* (Red harvest, 1946) and *Os subterrâneos da liberdade*

(The freedom underground, 1954), were among his most explicitly political works; they generally were not nearly as technically sophisticated as most of the modernist fiction in Latin America at the time. Amado's literary career changed in 1958 with the publication of *Gabriela, Clove and Cinnamon*. With this work, ironic humor entered into Amado's fiction in a significant way for the first time; this was his first satirical novel. The humorous scenes that occasionally marked his previous works are integrated into the novel's very texture.[5] This satire of Brazilian society is also a parody, in language and form, of colonial chronicles. As such, the novel contains archaic language in its chapter and section titles, as well as frequent enumerations. The main targets of Amado's satire are traditional sex roles and, in particular, the stereotypical roles of women.

After *Gabriela, Clove and Cinnamon*, Amado published many more novels. With all his work from the 1930s to the 1950s, he made a significant contribution to the modernization of the novel in Brazil and Latin America, independent of his commercial success.

## Graciliano Ramos

Ramos published most of his fiction before the rise of modernist fiction in Latin America in the mid-1940s. More of a stylist interested in narrative technique than Lins do Rêgo or Amado, Ramos played a key role in bringing modernist aesthetics to the Brazilian novel. One informed Brazilian critic has described Ramos as "an erudite version of the countryman's dialect of the Northeast, regionalism in classic form, slang of the zone and plebeian 'cuss words' carefully set down in the purest of Portuguese, with pronouns rigorously placed and exact grammatical usage."[6]

Ramos was born in 1892 into a more modest family than Lins do Rêgo or Amado, and was reared near Buique on the ranch of his grandparents. His childhood experiences on the *sertão* were important for his early fictions, which included *Caetés* (1933), *São Bernardo* (1934), *Anguish* (1936), and *Barren Lives* (1938). A more technically innovative book was *Insônia* (Insomnia, 1947). He died in 1953.

His first novel, *Caetés*, deals with a character named João Valério, the narrator-protagonist who is a bookkeeper in a commercial firm named Teixeira & Brother. He has an affair with Luisa, the wife of the firm's owner; João, too, aspires to be a writer and relates some of his own fictional work in the course of the novel. The novel deals with an Indian population, the Caetés, in a remote part of Brazil. It tells of the vicissitudes of the relationship between the protagonist and Luisa, as well his distracted attempts to write his novel. Luisa's husband receives a letter about the affair, becomes distraught, and commits suicide. At the end, João settles into life in the town and continues his work as an accountant in the firm, abandoning his novel. *Caetés* was received in Brazil, at the time of its publication, as the work of a significant artist, "not merely a documentation of northeastern life."[7]

*São Bernardo*, Ramos's second novel, tells of the story of the tragedy of Paulo Honório, a man who destroys the person he loves. In the process of ruthlessly building a great plantation, he also writes his memoir. The novel relates Paulo Honório's rise from the low life and jail to becoming the owner of the São Bernardo plantation. Once again, Ramos uses a first-person narrator, and his language is brief and direct.

In *Anguish,* Ramos creates yet another protagonist who is an aspiring writer; this one is a petty bureaucrat named Luís da Silva. This novel deals with Luís's intense love for Marina and his equally intense hatred for his rival Julião Tavares. The narrator-protagonist, who tells his own story, shares the pessimism of many of Ramos's other protagonists. One scholar has described this novel as "a complete study in frustration employing a maximum of dramatic tension."[8]

In *Barren Lives,* Ramos uses a structure different from that of his other novels. The novel's different chapters can be read as individual fragments or as part of the whole. Here, he uses the third person, lending the novel "epic" and "tragic" qualities.[9] Ramos also reveals social and political problems on the *sertão* without making his novel a direct political manifesto.[10]

Ramos was in his modernist mode when writing his volume of stories titled *Insônia.* They communicate a sense of unreality and are seemingly related to nightmares and insomnia. These are stories of tormented individuals. The title story, "Insomnia," is told in the first person and deals with a protagonist who seems to be sick. Here, as in several others in this volume, a clock is an important device. "Um ladrão" (A thief) communicates several levels of consciousness, as well as several different times in the past and present. This story involves an operation that the narrator-protagonist experiences in a hospital. "Luciana" tells of the methods a young girl invents in order to survive repressive parents; she resorts to living in a fantasy world and playacting. Another third-person narration occurs in "Minsk," which has a parrot and a young girl as the central characters. "Dois dedos" (Two fingers) deals with an encounter between a doctor and a governor who have not seen each other for 20 years. Their reunion turns into a debacle, for they have changed entirely and now have nothing in common. In "Silveira Pereira," Ramos uses a first-person narrator to tell the story of an aspiring young writer whose stories fail to interest another character in the story.

Ramos also published memoirs and a partial autobiography before his death in 1953. His fiction remains a testimony to his social commitment and his efforts to modernize literature in Brazil.

# Rachel de Queiroz

The fourth member of this northeastern quartet, Rachel de Queiroz, was both highly productive and technically sophisticated. She offers a feminine perspective to the social and political realities of this region of Brazil. Writing in the 1950s about these four novelists, one critic stated about de Queiroz that "certainly no other writer of the Northeast shows so great an understanding of maternal instinct and tenderness toward children, and, above all, so warm and generous a spirit toward all mankind."[11]

De Queiroz was born in 1910 and reared on her father's ranch in the *sertão*. As a child, she accepted the traditional role assigned to young women in the region, living a relatively isolated and submissive life in a society dominated by men. She was trained as a teacher but began writing at an early age, and by the age of 20 had already published her first novel, *O Quinze* (The year nineteen fifteen, 1930). She followed with *João Miguel* (John Michael,1932), *Caminho de pedras* (Stoney road,1937), *The Three Marías* (1939), and in 1948 came forth with a volume containing the first three of these works.

In her fiction of the 1930s, Rachel de Queiroz was fundamentally a traditionalist. *O Quinze,* set in the barren Brazilian landscape, presents desperate scenes of hunger and death. The action involves the migration of the locals from the area. The main themes are the cyclic drought of the land and the role of women in society. In *João Miguel,* there is more psychological depth in the author's consideration of the role of women. The central women in this novel are prostitutes, and de Queiroz analyses the situation, once again, of white masters and black slaves. The author continues her critique of women's roles in *Caminho de pedras*, a satire of the institution of marriage in Brazil. In *The Three Marías*, de Queiroz examines a woman throughout her life, dealing with the protagonist in more psychological depth than she did in any of her previous novels.

# Conclusion

Lins de Rêgo, Amado, Ramos, and de Queiroz made numerous contributions to the modernization of the Latin American novel that are comparable to those of Asturias, Yáñez and Carpentier. All seven of these novelists, writing in Spanish and Portuguese, desired to be considered more universal than their predecessors. In their early years, the Brazilians tended to be as overtly political as Asturias and Carpentier. Later, in the 1940s and 1950s, they began to exercise the right of invention as it was being used by writers of the Spanish language. Their use of modernist aesthetic principles was never as radical as those practiced by writers such as Asturias and Yáñez. Nevertheless, the four wrote landmark novels that will be remembered for their authors' interest in national politics, narrative technique, and universalizing effects. All four wrote fiction based on the transcendent regionalism associated with the universal writers of the Spanish language who were prominent in the 1940s, 1950s, and 1960s.

# Part 2

# The Modernist Boom

# 7

# *Introduction to the Boom*

## Introduction

The Boom represented the international recognition, during the 1960s, of the superb quality of Latin American fiction. The rise of Borges and modernist fiction since the 1940s had laid the groundwork for this acknowledgment of the outstanding writing of Gabriel García Márquez, Carlos Fuentes, Mario Vargas Llosa, and Julio Cortázar. Their work, along with the writing of José Donoso, Jorge Amado, João Guimarães Rosa, Salvador Garmendia, and others, produced a body of literature that many scholars consider without comparison in the Spanish language since Spain's Golden Age in the seventeenth century.

For the first time, Latin American writers enjoyed the privilege of dedicating themselves full time to writing. Indeed, by the late 1960s, most of the writers of the Boom were living in Europe and writing full time. García Márquez and Vargas Llosa were living in Barcelona, often visited there by Cortázar and Fuentes. Now, Latin American writers were true professionals; some of them were even enjoying the lifestyle of jet-setters.

The Boom of the Latin American novel in the 1960s was a result of the confluence of numerous institutions, individuals, and circumstances, among them the Cuban Revolution, Harper and Row publishers in the United States, the Spanish literary agent Carmen Balcells, the Spanish publishing firm Seix Barral, the rise of international Latin Americanism as an academic discipline, the publication of the magazine *Mundo Nuevo* in Paris, and the appearance of a brilliant translator, Gregory Rabassa. As José Donoso has documented in his *Historia personal del Boom,* Fuentes was central to making all these factors come together. Most of the writers of the Boom had been to literary soirées as guests at the Fuentes home in Mexico City, including Vargas Llosa and Donoso himself. The latter, in fact, lived and wrote in a bungalow in Fuentes's backyard for three years in the early 1960s.

Fuentes followed closely and supported the writing of one of the major novels of the Boom, Gabriel García Márquez's *One Hundred Years of Solitude*. García Márquez liked to chat about his work when it was in progress, and he found Fuentes the ideal friend while he was writing the novel in 1965 and 1966 and joining in Fuentes's Sunday soirées. Fuentes was also one of the few individuals to read the manuscript of *One Hundred Years of Solitude* before its publication, prompting him to write an article of considerable impact in the principal Spanish-language literary organ of the Boom, *Mundo Nuevo*.

# The Rise of the Boom

During the 1960s, an unprecedented conjunction of forces occurred in Latin American literature. At the outset of the decade, the Cuban Revolution became a rallying point for most Latin American intellectuals, and the writers of the Boom supported revolutionary ideals in the early 1960s. In fact, when Castro arrived triumphantly in Havana in January of 1960, Carlos Fuentes was waiting for him to offer his congratulations and support. García Márquez was also an early ally of the revolution, and soon thereafter Vargas Llosa and Cortázar offered their solidarity. Castro successfully made Havana a center of cultural activity for Latin American intellectuals during the 1960s, with the full support of the rising stars of the Boom. Each of them made numerous trips to Havana, and García Márquez continued his close contact with the island into the 1990s.

The American publishing firm of Harper and Row was important to the Boom because it published the major novels of these writers. For the first time, the most gifted novelists of Latin America had an immediate outlet and a broad readership in the United States. The modernist strategies these writers used, as well as the magic realism that virtually became the trademark of Latin American writing, appealed to a broad audience in the United States; and writers from Latin America with the talent to utilize these two elements well developed a vast readership in English. That following, in turn, helped enhance the international appeal of this writing in Latin America. García Márquez, for example, gained a broad readership in Europe, Latin America in general, and the United States before enjoying wide acceptance in Colombia, a nation far more traditional in its literary tastes than the remainder of Latin America or the United States. The symbolic moment in which the ideology of the Cuban Revolution and the politics of the Boom were united occurred in 1962 at a literary conference in Concepción, Chile. There, Fuentes declared to Donoso and other prominent Chilean intellectuals that the Latin American writer should be *engagé* and join in solidarity with the Cuban Revolution. As Donoso has explained in his history of the Boom, never before had he heard a writer express such political positions so stridently.[1]

In Spain, the work of literary agent Carmen Balcells and the Seix Barral publishing firm also contributed to the rise of the Boom. Balcells set high professional standards for Latin American writers and their writing that were unprecedented. In doing so, she was highly influential in the rise of Latin American novelists as full-time professional writers. Before Balcells, the vast majority of them were forced to operate as weekend writers while pursuing other professions in order to sustain themselves economically. Fuentes inherited a sense of writing as a full-time profession from his mentor, Alfonso Reyes, even though his upper-class family was skeptical that anyone could enjoy a successful career writing literature professionally. For Vargas Llosa and García Márquez, however, the very idea of being a full-time writer in Latin America seemed to be an unrealizable dream. The financial success of *One Hundred Years of Solitude* basically resolved the issue for García Márquez; for Vargas Llosa, the encouragement of Balcells in the late 1960s was very important. At the same time, the Seix Barral publishing firm in Barcelona not only published high-quality fiction but also managed to distribute it successfully throughout the Hispanic world. Since then, several multinational companies have done the same, but in the early 1960s, rarely was a contemporary Latin American novel well distributed across multiple national boundaries.

The magazine *Mundo Nuevo*, published in Paris and edited by the literary critic Emir Rodríguez Monegal, served not only as an important cultural organ for Latin American writers in general but also as a key outlet for the writers of the Boom. Articles by them or about their work appeared regularly. In 1967, just before the appearance of *One Hundred Years of Solitude*, Fuentes wrote his influential article in *Mundo Nuevo* praising it; a chapter of the novel was also printed in the magazine. With their novels distributed internationally from Barcelona and news of their work circulating globally from Paris, Latin American writers had a presence never before seen or even imagined.

# The Novels of the Boom

Some of the major novels of the Spanish language appeared during the years of the Boom. Indeed, works such as García Márquez's *One Hundred Years of Solitude*, Fuentes's *The Death of Artemio Cruz*, Vargas Llosa's *The Green House*, and Cortázar's *Hopscotch* are considered modern classics in the Hispanic world. At the same time, these and other works of the Boom are in the process of being canonized in American, European, and Latin American academia.

By the early 1960s, Latin American novelists were writing with a confidence and maturity unequaled in the literary history of the region. The reaffirmation of the right of invention established by Borges and the novelists of the 1940 clearly had had its effects upon the next generation of writers. Certainly no group of Latin American writers had ever confronted the enormous task of creating a Latin American literature with the same confidence, sophistication, and energy as was represented in the combined creative efforts of Fuentes, Vargas Llosa, Cortázar, and García Márquez. Their novels and other works of fiction of the early 1960s—some of which were as accomplished as the novels of the Boom—shared certain common threads.[2] The transformation of regionalism that had begun in the 1940s continued into the 1960s. The innovative narrative techniques of high modernism were extensively and intensely elaborated in novels of the Boom and Latin American fiction in general of the 1960s. By the end of the decade, in fact, Latin American writers had carried the possibility of narrative technique to its limits, elaborating such complex and challenging novels as Vargas Llosa's *Conversation in The Cathedral* (1969) and Fuentes's *A Change of Skin* (1967). The novelists of this period were also beginning to experiment with ways to engage actively the reader in the creative process; the most celebrated effort along these lines was Cortázar's *Hopscotch*, but other works of this type appeared with increasing frequency as the 1960s progressed.

The early major works associated with the Boom were Vargas Llosa's *The Time of the Hero* (given the Biblioteca Breve literary prize in 1962; published in 1963) and Fuentes's *The Death of Artemio Cruz* (1962). Vargas Llosa wrote *The Time of the Hero* in Paris, often sharing the manuscript with Cortázar. When he completed it, he attempted to get it published in Paris in French but failed. The French literary critic Claude Couffon served as an intermediary and managed to get a reading from the Spanish editor Carlos Barral. Barral's interest in the book and the subsequent award of the Biblioteca Breve prize contributed to Vargas Llosa exploding onto the literary scene in the 1960s. *La ciudad y los perros* (the original Spanish title of *The Time of the Hero*), in fact, was one of the few Latin American novels ever to have gained a wide readership throughout Latin America at the time of its publication.[3] With his first novel, Vargas Llosa was an instant celebrity at the age of 26. Fuentes achieved similar success with *The Death of Artemio Cruz*, although he already had gained a literary reputation in Mexico with the publication of his first novel, *Where the Air Is Clear* (1958). In terms of public recognition, Vargas Llosa was aided by the fact that *The Time of the Hero* was considered something of a scandal in Peru because of its irreverent critique of a renowned military school in Lima.

In Latin America, Cortázar's *Hopscotch* represented a literary revolution that seemed to spawn all sorts of other revolutions. This "antinovel," as Cortázar called it, represented a subversion of all traditional forms of art, including the novel. Cortázar's alter ego in the novel, a writer named Morelli, proposes radical changes in the novel form that eventually resulted, in fact, in the appearance of a broad range of postmodern novels in the late 1960s and beyond. *Hopscotch* was one of those works—like Borges's *Ficciones* before and García Márquez's *One Hundred Years of Solitude* after—that opened the door to wherever the writers' imagination might lead them. In addition, no other work of fiction from Latin America had ever extended such an explicit invitation to the reader to participate in the creative process. The engagement of the reader pioneered in *Hopscotch* became a common strategy in postmodern fiction of the late 1960s and 1970s.

The publication of *The Death of Artemio Cruz*, *The Time of the Hero*, and *Hopscotch* provided the first announcement of the Boom. After the appearance of these fine novels, even more accomplished books of fiction were produced in the 1960s, including *One Hundred Years of Solitude*, Vargas Llosa's *The Green House* (1965) and *Conversation in The Cathedral* (1969), Fuentes's *A Change of Skin* (1967) and *Birthday* (1969). José Donoso, who was closely associated with the writers of the Boom, published *The Obscene Bird of the Night* in 1970.

# Other Novelists of the 1960s

The enormous attention paid to the writers of the Boom, unfortunately, tended to overshadow the overall high quality of Latin American writing. For the reader of the entire range of Latin American fiction, the Boom represented the tip of the iceberg. Such talented writers as the Brazilians Clarice Lispector and João Guimarães Rosa; the Chileans José Donoso and Jorge Guzmán; the Venezuelans Salvador Garmendia and Adriano González León; the Colombians Manuel Mejía Vallejo, Manuel Zapata Olivella, and Héctor Rojas Herazo; the Cubans José Lezama Lima, Guillermo Cabrera Infante, and Severo Sarduy; the Argentinians Manuel Puig, David Viñas, and Héctor Libertella; and the Mexicans Fernando del Paso, José Emilio Pacheco, Salvador Elizondo, José Agustín, and Gustavo Sainz were often ignored in favor of more celebrated novelists.

These and other talented Latin American writers produced some of the most accomplished novels of the 1960s, including Lezama Lima's *Paradiso* (1966) and González León's *País portátil* (1968). Modernist fiction was at its zenith in Latin America, and a host of more experimental postmodern novels appeared, such as Elizondo's *Farabeuf* (1965), Cabrera Infante's *Three Trapped Tigers* (1967), and Puig's *Betrayed by Rita Hayworth* (1969).

# The Demise of the Boom

By the early 1970s, the unity among the writers of the Boom began to dissipate, and by the mid-1970s they were no longer personal friends and political allies. The phenomenon of the Boom had reached its end, even though each of the period's four major writers continued his stellar literary career.

In the late 1960s, when García Márquez, Vargas Llosa, and Donoso were living in Barcelona, Cortázar was in Paris and Fuentes spent most of his time in Mexico. During these years, the Boom was at its zenith, and the personal relationships among Fuentes, García Márquez, Vargas Llosa, Cortázar, and Donoso were at their best. In December 1968, García Márquez, Cortázar, and Fuentes boarded a train in Paris for Prague and then toured several Soviet-bloc countries. As well as being close friends, they formed a united front politically and aesthetically.

Despite the friendships, schisms among the writers of the Boom began to surface for both political and personal reasons. The first major public indication of growing political differences appeared with the celebrated case of the Cuban poet Heberto Padilla. When he was arrested for writing poetry that the Cuban government considered unacceptable, several of Latin America's most prominent intellectuals protested. Fuentes, Vargas Llosa, Donoso, and others signed a letter directed to Castro demanding the release of Padilla. Over the ensuing years, García Márquez and Cortázar remained firmly aligned with the Cuban leader, while Fuentes, Donoso, and Vargas Llosa have been more distanced and occasionally critical.

The last time the writers of the Boom were all together, in fact, was in 1970 in France. To attend a theater festival in Avignon that included a presentation of Fuentes's play *El tuerto es rey*, Fuentes, García Márquez, Vargas Llosa and Donoso, along with the Spanish writer Juan Goytisolo, stayed at a home near Avignon owned by Cortázar. In Avignon the six made plans for their involvement in the quarterly magazine of criticism *Libre*, which Goytisolo edited. According to him, the venture should have welded these writers together but it became, in fact, a weapon pitting them against each other, until in the end they were enemies.[4] Goytisolo has explained the situation in more detail as follows. *Libre* was financed by Albina de Boisrourray, a young, beautiful, and wealthy woman with a passion for literature and cinema. When Goytisolo met with Fuentes and the other writers in Avignon, he intended to publish a magazine that would support the Cuban regime from the outside and also strengthen the position of intellectuals who, like Padilla, were struggling inside Cuba for freedom of expression and real democracy. But their earlier differences over Cuba and Padilla resulted in further divisions among the writers of the Boom. Since the Avignon meeting, the friendships and alliances among Latin American writers have been defined, in many cases, by positions for or against the Cuban government.

# The Boom in the 1990s

The writers of what was the 1960s Boom have few associations among themselves today. Cortázar, who had maintained personal relationships with the other three, died in 1984. Fuentes and García Márquez, who had become friends in the early 1960s in Mexico City, have maintained their friendship throughout the decades. They both own homes in Mexico City and frequently socialize when they are both in the Mexican capital. Vargas Llosa and Fuentes own homes in London, where Vargas Llosa lives year-round and Fuentes resides six months a year. Political differences, however, have created barriers between them. Vargas Llosa has become too politically conservative for Fuentes and many other Latin American intellectuals. Vargas Llosa and García Márquez also have distanced themselves from one another and have not been on speaking terms since the early 1970s.

By the 1990s, the impressive visibility of the Latin American writer of the 1960s Boom had been matched by that of several women writers. The rise of the Chilean Isabel Allende and the Mexican Laura Esquivel (whose book sales have surpassed some of the writings of the Boom) has proven that talented women writers, too, can be celebrity figures in Latin America.

# 8

# *The Novels of Carlos Fuentes*

## Introduction

Carlos Fuentes decided early in his life—in the 1950s—that the Mexican novel needed modernization and that it was the task of his generation to write the modern Latin American novel. As a youth, he was an avid reader of Borges, from whom he learned valuable lessons about the use of time and space. Fuentes was also an enthusiastic reader of modernist fiction in general, from Carpentier to Dos Passos, Faulkner, and Kafka. By the 1990s, he had published over 20 books of fiction.

Among the leading writers of the Boom, Fuentes was the novelist who contributed the most to emphasizing the social and political responsibility of the Latin American writer. Like the others—particularly Mario Vargas Llosa—he took from Jean-Paul Sartre the idea of the writer as an *engagé,* a politically committed individual. Fuentes was perhaps the first radical political voice among these writers; in the later stages of the Boom and particularly after the early 1970s, Cortázar and García Márquez were more vocally leftist than Fuentes.

Fuentes was the child of Mexican diplomats who, in his youth, lived in the United States, Mexico, Chile, and Argentina. Consequently, as a writer and intellectual, he is the consummate man of the Americas. He was not only reading the modernists of the West at an early age but also writing as a young adolescent. In 1945, at the age of 17, he and his family moved from Buenos Aires to Mexico City. Fuentes spent his youth and much of his adult life in the Mexican capital until the late 1960s. Since then, he has lived regularly in Mexico but has regularly alternated his residence between London and Mexico City, with frequent stays in the United States.

In Mexico, Fuentes's generation of young intellectuals of the 1950s felt the dual need to modernize Mexican literature and to define Mexican identity in a universal context. The modernization of Mexican fiction was already afoot, of course, with the novels of Agustín Yáñez; and *The Edge of the Storm* had already been published when Fuentes's generation was clamoring for a more modern Mexican literature. Along with Yáñez, they were interested in the technical possibilities of modernism. In addition, however, they viewed modernization as taking the Mexican novel out of the rural context of Yáñez and Rulfo, and urbanizing the settings and topics of Mexican writing. They looked to Borges and Mexican short-story writer Juan José Arreola as models of how to deal with physical space in fiction; they looked to Octavio Paz as the writer who, in his 1950 essay *The Labyrinth of Solitude*, had spoken most eloquently about Mexican identity. Fuentes's first novel, *Where the Air Is Clear* (1958), is a product of the interest in both modernization and the exploration of a new, more universal, definition of Mexican identity.

# Major Novels

Fuentes has published a vast oeuvre of high-quality fiction, including at least a dozen novels that are broadly read in Spanish and other languages. Nevertheless, Fuentes's most recognized works, by both the general public and critics, are *The Death of Artemio Cruz* (1962), *A Change of Skin* (1967), and *Terra Nostra* (1975).

*The Death of Artemio Cruz* was both Fuentes's first contribution to the Boom and his critique of the modern state that had developed in Mexico. An omniscient narrator constructs various time periods in the 12 narrative segments that take place from 1889 to 1959. This partially historical novel of twentieth-century Mexico loses any sense of chronological storytelling through the use of various strategies. On the one hand, these dated and historical sections do not appear in chronological order; on the other, the sections narrated by "yo" (I) and "tú" (you) create a variety of atemporal effects. When the "tú" narrator states "lo que pasará ayer" ("that which will happen yesterday"), the temporal oxymoron has the effect of destroying the Western concept of linear time; the important changes in this novel are temporal by nature.

In *The Death of Artemio Cruz*, Fuentes once again fictionalizes several of his ideas about Mexican identity that he and Octavio Paz had been popularizing since the publication of Paz's *The Labyrinth of*

*Solitude* in 1950. Consequently, several passages of *The Death of Artemio Cruz* portray the Mexican as the heir of Malinche in Mexico. The most significant identity for protagonist Cruz is that of survivor: his only consistent and certain affirmation on his deathbed is "yo sobreviví" ("I survived").

The idea for *A Change of Skin* had been suggested near the middle of Fuentes's first novel, *Where the Air Is Clear*, when he uses the phrase "change of skin." The new novel, like many of Fuentes's works, negates linear time and, in addition, looks to the future. The basic referents in this novel are Palm Sunday, April 11, 1965, and the town of Cholula in Mexico. The four main characters—Javier, Elizabeth, Franz, and Isabel—make a trip by car to Cholula, the site of one of Mexico's most renowned pyramids. But the novel introduces different times and places, including Spain during the Inquisition, German concentration camps, Hiroshima, and Vietnam. Continuing his search for the eternal moment suggested in some of his previous work, Fuentes strives for the experience of creative re-creation. *A Change of Skin* ends, however, with Javier in a state of postmodern exhaustion.

*Terra Nostra* is Fuentes's major and culminating reading of Latin American culture and history, and it is, in addition, his major work dealing with identity, knowledge, and the novel itself. Fuentes has been concerned with the culture, history, and identity of the Americas since his youth. *Where the Air Is Clear, The Death of Artemio Cruz,* and *A Change of Skin* were major projects regarding these issues. In addition to the particulars of Latin American history, Fuentes is concerned with how history, culture, and identity are constructed and then understood. He had concluded well before writing *Terra Nostra* that history should be understood not as the compilation of immutable truths but as a living world in transformation.

With his writing of *Terra Nostra*, begun at the same time he was discovering Foucault, Fuentes started to explore history conceptualized beyond the terms that he, Vargas Llosa, and a host of other Latin American writers had been using in their respective historical inquiries. The historical questions of *Terra Nostra* certainly concern issues well beyond those found in Latin American empirical experience. Fuentes utilized Foucault's observations about the major functions of history in Western culture, such as memory, myth, transmission of the word and example, vehicle of tradition, critical awareness of the present, decipherment of humanity's destiny, anticipation of the future, and promise of return.[1] These functions provide Fuentes with material at the same time that he critiques the traditional roles of empirical history.

The concept of history that Fuentes writes against in *Terra Nostra* has its roots in nineteenth-century ideas of history that were still predominant ideological constructs in Mexico and much of Latin America in the twentieth century. The Romantic conception of history as progress, promoted by numerous Mexican institutions, including the PRI, and which Fuentes critiqued initially in *Where the Air Is Clear* and *The Death of Artemio Cruz*, is subverted in *Terra Nostra* by the novel's structure. In *Terra Nostra* (and essays written in the 1970s), Fuentes fictionalizes a more rational medieval past than the historical record of orthodox Christianity, as well as an irrational future represented by a boiling Seine River, multiple births on the streets of Paris, and other equally inexplicable events that occur in a future beyond 1975, when *Terra Nostra* was published.

The history represented in *Terra Nostra* also reveals traces of a pre-Hispanic understanding of history and time. Western history, as written since the Bible, has traditionally been linear; pre-Hispanic history of indigenous cultures, as symbolized by the Aztec sundial, is cyclical. The Maya, Aztec, and other indigenous civilizations expected history to repeat itself in cycles; the reader's experience of history and time in *Terra Nostra* is comparable to this concept.

History, culture, and identity are closely related concepts in *Terra Nostra*. Both traditional linear (biblical) history and cyclical (Greek, Aztec, Nietzchean) concepts of history are explored and ultimately negated in the novel. With this critique and subversion of the well-known concepts of historiography, Fuentes questions both traditional Latin American ideas about cultural essence and any possibility of history as truth.

# The Cycles of Fuentes's Fiction

Fuentes himself considers all his fiction as one work, a lifetime writing project he has organized around 14 cycles, which he has entitled "La edad del tiempo" and which he considers to be a lengthy reflection on time.[2] The four works that Fuentes calls "El mal del tiempo" comprise the first of these 14 cycles, and they deal with the problem of time itself. In them, any sense of Western linear time is blurred; in different ways, they undermine and destroy time. The four books in this first cycle are *Aura* (1962), *Birthday* (1969), *Distant Relations* (1980), and *Constancia and Other Stories for Virgins* (1990). With *Aura*, Fuentes begins his attack on time, initiated with the use of a second-person narrator combined with an enigmatic future tense that both negates and destroys time. In this novel, the protagonist, Felipe Montero, is a twentieth-century character who becomes fused with a nineteenth-century historical character; as such, he is one of two characters doubled in this novel, with Aura being the other. In *Birthday*, Fuentes develops some of the experiments of *Aura* in a more radical way. Some of the concepts suggested as themes and possibilities in Fuentes's other fiction are put in practice in this book, his most hermetic and experimental novel. Set in London, the story deals with a multiple set of identities: George; his son, Georgie; his wife; characters named Nuncia and Nino; and the thirteenth-century Averroist philosopher Siger of Brabant. Their constantly transforming identities and distant relations associate and overlap in the most enigmatic fashion of any of Fuentes's novels until *Terra Nostra*. *Distant Relations* expands and develops several of the problems found in *Aura*. The complex plot tells of a Heredia family in Mexico attempting to find its connections with Heredias in France. One of Fuentes's most accomplished novels, *Distant Relations* deals with the Latin American cultural heritage that came from France, as *Terra Nostra* had done with Spain. *Distant Relations* suggests much about Fuentes as writer and his interests in literature, for this is a book that promotes the idea that living, in the end, is predicated on the act of telling a story. In this novel, culture is recognized not only in a multicultural world but also in a culturally interdependent one, even though relations may be, at a first glance, distant ones. *Constancia and Other Stories for Virgins* also deals with distant relations, which are elaborated in five stories located in a variety of settings ranging from the old historical center of Mexico City to Savannah, Georgia.

The second of Fuentes's 14 cycles consists solely of *Terra Nostra*, the foundational novel for the total cycle of "La edad del tiempo." With *Terra Nostra*, time is set in motion in Fuentes's cycle, beginning with the Western and Native American roots of the Americas. *Terra Nostra* both incorporates and negates Western linear time as well as Aztec circular time. It is Fuentes's most elaborate and complex version of the theme of distant relations.

His third cycle, "El tiempo romántico," consists of three novels, one of which Fuentes has written, *The Campaign*, and two more that he has planned to write. With *The Campaign*, Fuentes continues from the foundation established in *Terra Nostra* to the period in the early nineteenth century when Latin America was fighting for independence. It relates the story of Balthasar Bustos, a Latin American child of the Enlightenment who is obsessed with a woman and who joins the revolutionary forces that forged independence. The novel follows the independence movement in the Río del Plata, in the region of today's Bolivia, in Chile, in Peru, up the west coast of South America to Colombia and Venezuela, and finally in Veracruz, Mexico. It is Fuentes's only novel set in Latin American nations other than Mexico, but it is one of several works with characters in search of origins and truth.

In his fourth cycle, "El tiempo revolucionario," Fuentes fictionalizes the period of the early-twentieth-century Mexican Revolution with two novels, *Old Gringo* and another one in the planning stages. *Old Gringo* is the story of two Americans in Mexico, Ambrose Bierce and Harriet Winslow, and it is an example of Fuentes at his storytelling best. In his fiction, individuals always live in relationship to others, and their actions affect others; in *Old Gringo*, the destinies of the three main characters are fully dependent upon others. As is especially evident in *Hydra Head*, they do not act as individuals with a particular identity, but they play roles that are the fulfillment of an identity: Harriet Winslow takes the role of the American woman who is the daughter of an American; the old gringo assumes the role of the American dreamer and writer; Tomás Arroyo plays the role of the proto-Mexican in the Mexican Revolution. They can play other roles, too, in the course of constant substitutions. The most intense of these games of substitutions is a scene in which Harriet dances with Arroyo thinking of her father, while Arroyo dances with her imagining his mother. Like *Terra Nostra*, *Old Gringo* is really a novel about language and writing. Throughout, reality is portrayed not as it is observed in the empirical world around the characters but as it is conceived within the bounds of their language, their imaginations, and their stories. As in *Distant Relations*, in *Old Gringo* the power of storytelling predominates over empirical reality.

Fuentes's fifth cycle consists of just one novel, *Where the Air Is Clear*. It deals with modern Mexico in the 1940s and 1950s and the issue of national identity. In itself, the modernity of Mexico is fictionalized within a context of rapid capitalization and promotion of industrial and technological "progress." This progress is fictionalized in the successes and failures of individuals, with their respective ascents and descents in Mexican society. National identity, in fact, is frequently conceptualized in this novel in opposition to progress: the modern Mexican is portrayed as an uprooted individual who has lost any sense of past and identity. The modern Mexican is also the citizen of the novel's setting in Mexico City: a culturally complex and historically bound urban area.

*The Death of Artemio Cruz* is the sixth of the 14 cycles. In it, Fuentes continues his practice of simultaneously constructing historical time and destroying the subjective time of the individual. Some of the issues and themes of *Terra Nostra* are more fully developed in *The Death of Artemio Cruz* than they had been in *Where the Air Is Clear* or *The Good Conscience*. As in *The Good Conscience*, the matter of individual choice is extremely important in *The Death of Artemio Cruz*. The protagonist's failure as a human being is portrayed as the culmination of a series of poor moral decisions, just as one of Spain's historical problem lies, according to Fuentes, in its decision to isolate itself from the Europe of the Renaissance and the Enlightenment.

The seventh cycle is a novel Fuentes expects to be titled *Los años con Laura Díaz* (The years with Laura Díaz), which the author visualizes as a companion novel to *The Death of Artemio Cruz*.[3] The woman who is the protagonist functions as a counterpart to Artemio Cruz.

The eighth cycle is titled "Dos educaciones" and consists of the novels *The Good Conscience* and *Holy Place*. In both works, the protagonist passes through a rite of passage. In *The Good Conscience*, it is the young Jaime Ceballos who suffers the experience of growing up in the traditional and provincial society of Guanajuato. This novel focuses on the Ceballos family, which is depicted by Fuentes the historian as incarnating the history of Guanajuato, which is combined with a strong sense of the development of a new oligarchy after the Mexican Revolution. The protagonist of *Holy Place*, Guillermo Nervo, is older than most fictional characters in the bildungsroman: he is the 29-year-old son of a celebrity actress who frequently overshadows him, causing an identity crisis. The only significant action of *Holy Place*, however, is the act of transformation.

The ninth cycle of Fuentes's fiction, "Los días enmascarados," consists of four books of short stories. The "masked days" of the title were holidays at the very end of the Aztec calendar, and they appear throughout Fuentes's work. The four volumes in this ninth cycle are *Los días enmascarados, Cantar de ciegos, Burnt Water*, and one more volume to be written, *La frontera de cristal*.

The tenth cycle, "El tiempo político," consists of one published novel, *Hydra Head*, and two forthcoming novels, *El sillón del águila* and *El camino a Texas*. They represent yet another concept of time—political time. In the first volume of this cycle, *Hydra Head*, political time is fundamentally the linear time of the spy thriller. The protagonist Félix Maldonado, an overly punctual bureaucrat, becomes unwillingly involved in a plot to assassinate the president of Mexico, as well as in a plot of international intrigue concerning Mexico's oil reserves.

The title of the eleventh cycle is "Cambìo de pìel," which is also the title of the one novel in it, *A Change of Skin*. In the novel, the past, the present, and the future exist here and now. An opening section moves back and forth, from one paragraph to the next, between the twentieth-century travel of the four main characters and the six-teenth-century conquest of Mexico by Hernán Cortés. In this lengthy and complex novel, Fuentes pursues the past time and place of pre-Columbian civilizations.

The twelfth of Fuentes's cycles consists solely of the novel *Christopher Unborn*. The idea of his 14 cycles of fiction developed while he was writing *Christopher Unborn* when he was a visiting professor at Dartmouth College in the early 1980s. One of Fuentes's most innovative works, *Christopher Unborn*, is also one of his most lengthy and ambitious novels, with most obvious parentage in *A Change of Skin* and *Terra Nostra*. Here, a return to origins takes on a different meaning: the narrator, Cristóbal, tells the story on January 6, 1992, from the womb of his mother, Angeles, who has conceived him in 1992 in Acapulco (also identified as Kafkapulco). As in the story "Apollo and the Whores" in *The Orange Tree*, Fuentes imagines a postmodern Mexico of the future that has trivialized not only its national myths and its institutions but also its very identity. *Christopher Unborn* is Fuentes's most irreverent fictional critique of the modern state of Mexico. The questioning of the nation's modernization found in *Where the Air Is Clear* and *The Death of Artemio Cruz* culminates, in *Christopher Unborn*, in images of a nation lost in the garbage and defecation that are the by-products of its own development.

The thirteenth cycle, "El tiempo actual," consists of three works, two of which have yet to be published. *Diana, the Goddess Who Hunts Alone* (1994) is Fuentes's semiautobiographical account of an affair he had with an American actress in the 1960s. Nevertheless, its real topic is not a love affair with a woman, but Fuentes's lifetime love affair with literature and writing.

The fourteenth cycle is based on a book of fiction, *The Orange Tree*, that could be considered either a loosely organized novel or a volume of short stories. The central image is the orange tree, which provides unity to the volume. Although not a common image in Fuentes's fiction, the orange had appeared before in *Hydra Head* and *Constancia and Other Stories for Virgins*. The final work in the cycle of "La edad del tiempo," this book is best read as a five-chapter novel rather than as a volume of five short stories. The constant image of the orange tree and the consistency of themes invite the reader to consider it a novel.

# Conclusion

The 14 cycles of Fuentes's fiction represent a major contribution to the modern novel in Latin American and to the Boom; they also represent one of the most significant bodies of literature to have been created by a Latin American writer since the colonial period and the founding of this region's literature. A vast body of work in time and space, it is set in all of the Hispanic world, from Spain to the Americas, from Argentina to the border between Mexico and the United States, and it represents a rewriting of history from Roman times to the present.

In this total work, Fuentes explores many of the issues synthesized in *Terra Nostra*. Fuentes's ficton in general, like *Terra Nostra*, exhibits a constant belief in the power of imagination as a value in itself. Liberation always returns, sooner or later, to imagination. After imagination, Fuentes values the power of ideas over other forces, such as the economic or the sexual.

Much of Fuentes's fiction explores the spaces and times of transformation and those forces that transform individuals, cultures, and societies. Many of his novels are located precisely at a period of change; for example, *The Campaign* is located temporally at the key moment of transformation of the Latin American nations from colony to republic. Similarly, *Terra Nostra* takes place during the conquest and colonization of the Americas, and *Christopher Unborn* during the postmodernization of the North American Free Trade Agreement.[4]

# 9

# The Novels of Julio Cortázar

## Introduction

Julio Cortázar was the intellectual father figure of the Boom and for the writers of the Boom themselves. In the 1950s, when the other writers of the group were still struggling to create their first works of fiction, Cortázar was already a venerated short-story writer. Indeed, several of his most celebrated stories were published in the 1950s.

Cortázar's already elevated stature among Latin American intellectuals and writers rose even more when he published *Hopscotch* in 1963. Never attaining the broad popular appeal of García Márquez or Vargas Llosa, Cortázar was considered, nevertheless, a giant among intellectual figures in Latin America. He was also one of the most consistently revolutionary voices on the Left, not only as a supporter of Castro in the 1960s but also of other leftist causes in the 1970s and 1980s, including the Sandinistas in Nicaragua.

In the 1960s, of course, the novelists of the Boom and many other writers in Latin America grappled with questions of political engagement and the revolutionary role of the writer. Cortázar was one of the writers who thought and wrote most deliberately on this subject—in essays, fiction, and other writings. In an interview done with Luis Harss in the mid-1960s, in fact, Cortázar stated that the more he assumed his role as a revolutionary writer, the less success he expected to achieve in his role as novelist. When he died in 1984, he had published over 30 books, including fiction, essays, and other creative works that escape genre boundaries. His work has strongly affected three generations of Latin American writers and has been seminal for both modern and postmodern fiction written in Latin America since the late 1960s.

Cortázar was born of Argentine parents in Brussels and moved to Argentina at the age of four. He lived in Argentina until moving to

France in 1951, where he spent the remainder of his life. He was the first of the writers of the Boom to pass away.

# Major Novels

Cortázar's major novels are *Hopscotch* (1963), *62: A Model Kit* (1968), and *A Manual for Manuel* (1973), although *Hopscotch* has been, by far, the work of greatest impact. All three are relatively complex and challenging novels that generally have attracted scholars and only the most sophisticated amateur readers.

The very structure of *Hopscotch* was revolutionary in Latin America in 1963 because it offers the possibility of reading at least three different novels, as Cortázar explains in a prefatory note after the title page. The first of these novels consists of chapters 1 through 56, which tell the story of Horacio Oliveira, a bohemian Argentine expatriate in Paris, and his relationship with a woman named La Maga. (Chapters 1–36 take place in Paris.) Oliveira lives in constant emotional crisis and does not seem capable of understanding either himself or his role in life, despite his sophisticated intellectual repertoire. His physical, romantic, and intellectual wanderings lead him to emotional and moral dead ends that eventually take him to Buenos Aires, where he continues his quest. (Chapters 37–56 take place in Buenos Aires.) Once in his homeland, he connects with his old friend Traveler and Traveler's wife, Talita. The three of them join a circus and engage in increasingly unorthodox activities and relationships. They eventually end up in an insane asylum, and the denouement offers an ambiguous situation in which Oliveira might or might not commit suicide. This first novel within *Hopscotch*, then, relates the story of Oliveira in a basically chronological fashion.

The first novel, if it were the complete text of an entire novelistic work, would be an attractive and intriguing fiction in the modernist vein, replete with its use of multiple points of view, fragmented structure, and language play associated with the strategems of modernism. As a modernist text, the first novel contains the characteristic search for the ineffable and the fascination with ambiguity as a value in itself.

The principal theme of chapters 1 to 56 is the quest.[1] Read as such, they constitute a novel of Oliveira's search for some kind of authenticity or substantive meaning in life. The novel begins with the question "¿Encontraría La Maga?" ("Would I find La Maga?"), thus announcing a search as the novel's point of departure. Indeed, the ongoing search for an authentic relationship with La Maga constitutes a large portion of the story in Paris. In addition, Oliveira's search is played out on a variety of other levels: as a metaphysical search, as a search for intellectual superiority, as a search for true artistic expression. In the end, his quest is inconclusive and leads him to both absurdly ridiculous situations and impending suicide.

The second novel contained in *Hopscotch*, also proposed in the author's prefatory note, consists of chapters 1 through 56, as well as 99 additional chapters that appear as 57 through 155. But these chapters do not appear in numerical order; rather, the reader jumps back and forth between chapters 1 and 56 and the new "expendable" chapters. Consequently, the novel begins with the following chapters: 73, 1, 116, 3, 84, 4, etc. In this second novel, Oliveira's story is expanded; several chapters further develop his story in Paris and Buenos Aires. In this novel, however, there are also numerous chapters dealing with subjects such as literature, art, philosophy, and the like, as well as a few short narratives that, on a first reading, seem like non sequiturs to the novel. With more consideration, however, it becomes evident that all these diverse elements have their respective functions in the novel.

Some of these playful fragments have the function of distancing the reader from the events at hand, inviting the reader to pause and reflect on the actions and ideas in a fashion comparable to Brechtian theater. Occasional comical passages also serve the same function. The long-term strategy with this distancing effect is to invite the reader of this second novel to reflect not only on the actions and characters but also on the novel form itself, as well as on the assumptions of readers and writers of fiction in general. Paradoxically, then, the most playful and apparently frivolous aspects of the novel turn out to be the most provocative and perhaps even revolutionary.

More important, the expendable chapters introduce a writer figure named Morelli and his theory of the novel. His theories appear as "Morelliana" or in a variety of other modes, including discussions of Morelli by other characters. Oliveira is a great admirer of Morelli; Oliveira and his cohorts in Paris, for example, are enthusiasts of avant-garde art in general and Morelli's unorthodox and even revolutionary theories in particular. Morelli questions not only the assumptions of the realist novel but also many of the operations of modernist fiction as well. He invites writers to undermine Western concepts of representation and time and, similarly, the very idea of linearity and plot. But one of his most radical proposals is for an entirely new role for the reader—as an active ("macho") participant. The postmodern reader of much of the innovative fiction that has been published in Latin American since *Hopscotch* is fundamentally Morelli's idea of the active reader.

In addition to proposing radical, new roles for the reader, the second reading of *Hopscotch* reveals an undermining of the very concept of author.[2] Lucille Kerr has argued convincingly that *Hopscotch* poses questions about the figure of the author and about the attribution of authorship.[3] One also finds evidence that this book's propositions about the author's authority both affirms and undermines authorial privileges. In this second reading of *Hopscotch*, the figure of the author seems to reclaim its own privilege under the names of several authors—Cortázar, Morelli, and others. By the end of the second reading, authorial figures and the very concept of authority are questioned.

A third reading of *Hopscotch* is more implied than clearly delineated, because it is only hinted at in the author's prefatory note. Cortázar suggests that the third reading is one the reader constructs; this is the radical novelistic adventure of the type proposed by Morelli. This form of reading generates the truly open novel that Cortázar seems to desire, but that is never actually attained in the first or second readings.

The second and third readings offered in *Hopscotch* necessarily bring to bear yet another important subject of this novel: language itself. On the one hand, the implied author seems disgusted with the limits and the treachery of language. Cortázar's critique is accompanied by innovative experiments with language that range from the amusing to apparent incoherence. Cortázar's challenge of accepted beliefs includes questioning orthodox language, but his exploration of language goes beyond critique and challenge. It also implies a radical proposition about how we use language to think and how language affects our everyday habits and customs.

Indeed, every aspect of the more complete (second and third) readings of *Hopscotch* inevitably bring the reader back to questioning the very fundamentals of Western culture, writing, and even thought. With this novel, Cortázar opened the door for two generations of postmodern fiction writers in Latin America, and also explored the possibilities and limits of radically undermining some of the most venerable assumptions of Western culture and thinking. Among these assumptions is what Cortázar (and Fuentes) considered the Western tendency to conceive of everything in dualistic terms. Manichaean thought, for Cortázar and Fuentes, is one of the Western traditions in most need of radical subversion. This radical aesthetic and political program becomes the new literary and ideological program of much postmodern fiction published in Latin America after the appearance of *Hopscotch*.

In chapter 62 of *Hopscotch*, Morelli suggests the possibility of creating a novel on the basis of random notes and observations. This is basically a postmodern idea that Cortázar himself pursued in *62: A Model Kit*, a work in which even the very concepts of character and plot are placed into doubt and in which "entities" (who often appear more as abstractions than characters who represent human beings) are caught up in a pattern of events that seem to occur at random in four places: London, Paris, Vienna, and "the City." Like *Hopscotch*, *62: A Model Kit* contains an element of search, although this one is more abstract and intangible. A character named Juan searches for Helene, a character whose identity is necessarily ambiguous: she could be a homosexual, a vampire, or a being defined by others.

In *Hopscotch*, chance plays a major role for the characters and the reader; chance appears as an important theme in *62: A Model Kit*. Characters and actions seem to develop simultaneously, with no regard for the rules of logic or order. A character named Monsieur Ochs makes dolls that contain objects that the purchasers are not aware of in advance. Once opened, the dolls also reveal apparently symbolic meanings to the characters. Many of the characters' actions related to the games of chance in the novel are either illogical or ludic.

In *62: A Model Kit*, Cortázar carries out some of the operations of fiction that were only radical proposals in *Hopscotch*. Here, Cortázar is practicing the postmodern fiction proposed in the earlier novel, creating entirely new postmodern concepts of character and space in fiction, which become abstract and undefinable entities. The characters operate in Paris, London, and Vienna (which, taken together, Cortázar calls the "zona"), as well as a spatial entity known as the "ciudad," which is an abstract zone as well as the three cities. Mi paredro, on the other hand, is an abstract entity who functions like a character, even though this abstract character is more like a double of several characters than a real person.

*A Manual for Manuel* is a continuation of Cortázar's radical and postmodern writing, but here his revolutionary political agenda is more explicit. Far from the abstract literary and linguistic experiments of his earlier novels, Cortázar now portrays revolutionaries in the realm of easily recognizable action, the world of urban guerrillas. *A Manual for Manuel* is the story of a political kidnapping in Paris. The central character, Andrés, must choose between violent guerrilla action and a nonviolent approach that might be interpreted as complicity with a powerful and violent ruling order. This postmodern text may be read as a novel only with the most liberal and broad definition of the genre in mind, for it is a book that consists of a multiplicity of texts that Andrés and his friends put together for the next generation—represented by Manuel. Consequently, the novel contains newspaper clippings with news about real events, including torture in Vietnam and violence in Europe.

In this work, Cortázar places before the reader real political questions that were debated by the writers of the Boom and others throughout Latin America in the late 1960s and early 1970s. The case of Cuban poet Heberto Padilla, who was jailed by Fidel Castro in 1971 for writing "antirevolutionary" poetry, was central to these debates. This case, which was articulated by the intellectuals as an issue of freedom of expression and human rights—polarized the novelists of the Boom and many other Latin American writers (see chapter 8). In addition, the election of Salvador Allende in Chile, the subsequent military coup, and the rise of a series of military regimes in Latin America all produced political turmoil and heated political debate among Latin American intellectuals.

This scenario in the early 1970s and political questions such as these are the essential background for an informed reading of *A Manual for Manuel*, but they are only the surface political texture for Cortázar. As in much of his fiction, Cortázar invites the reader to think beyond the most immediate political questions to find radical, new approaches to the broader issues. The essence of revolutionary change in *A Manual for Manuel*, then, is to be found in how one approaches language, sexuality, and ways of thinking. Both Cortázar and the character Andrés engage in an examination of writing and language, and their methods are as radical as those found in *Hopscotch*. Andrés and a character named Lonstein question traditional sexual mores and taboos.

As in *Hopscotch*, chance plays an important role in this novel. For Cortázar, chance was a constant theme because it questions the causality of logic and reason, thus denying, in a way, the very basis of Western thought. Western Logos was a continual target for Cortázar's critiques, and he saw this questioning as one of his most profoundly revolutionary acts.

Erotic play operates in *A Manual for Manuel* as an exploration of liberation and a breaking of social norms. The novel presents eroticism in a variety of facets, each angle representing a variation on the theme.[4] Cortázar explores a variety of erotic alternatives, beginning with the heterosexual conjugal play of Patricio and Susana, Manuel's parents. Andrés and Ludmilla represent the more casual approach to sexual relationships and their duration. Ludmilla later enters into intimate relations with Marcos, and Andrés with Francine. It is evident that for Andrés a multiplicity of erotic acts are the means of liberation. Cortázar also makes allusions to male and female homosexuality.

As Tittler points out, the field of play in *A Manual for Manuel* encompasses more than eroticism.[5] Three other types of play—the comic, the absurd, and a generally playful outlook—also operate in the novel. Characters are often placed in absurd situations, such as when two characters are watching a movie and facing a blank brick wall. The comic element is frequently evoked through humorous interchanges of dialogue among the characters. Their humor is generally based either on the juxtaposition of literary and vulgar language, or on the playful transgression of societal norms.

By the time Cortázar published *A Manual for Manuel* in 1973, he had basically abandoned his career as a "novelist" per se. *A Manual for Manuel* is a "novel" only in the broadest and loosest sense of the genre; in it Cortázar is far more interested in exploring the political possibilities of writing in general than in the formal or thematic possibilities of the "novel." In this sense, *A Manual for Manuel* is both the culminating postmodern project announced by Cortázar (and Morelli) in *Hopscotch* and his last "novel."

## Other Novels and Writings

Besides *Hopscotch*, *62: A Model Kit*, and *A Manual for Manuel*, Cortázar wrote two other novels, much short fiction, and several other books that escape simple genre definition. He wrote the novel *El examen* in 1950 in Argentina, but it was not published until 1986 (two years after his death). His first published novel was *The Winners*, which appeared in the original Spanish as *Los premios* in 1958. His short fiction brought him a broad and loyal readership. Many scholars consider him a better short-story writer than novelist, and most would agree that he is one of the major short-story writers of the century in the Spanish language.

*El examen* is of interest more as a historical object—as the first novel Cortázar wrote—than as a novel itself. In the late 1940s, when Cortázar wrote it, he and his cohorts were under attack by a faction of Peronists—followers of Juan Perón, the populist Argentine president—for being too European and elitist in literary outlook. Victoria Ocampo's magazine *Sur* was promoting a universal rather than nationalistic view of literature, which was a concept that appealed to Cortázar, as it did to all the writers of the Boom in the 1940s and 1950s. Set in this demoralizing atmosphere, *El examen* provides a brief glance at the lives of two couples in Buenos Aires. They talk at great length about the present and future of Argentina, which is literally crumbling under their feet as they wander the streets of Buenos Aires. An inexplicable and all-encompassing mist surrounds them as Juan and his fiancée leave for Europe, just as Cortázar himself did in 1950.

The setting of *The Winners* is a ship and a sea cruise that never gets beyond the Río de la Plata. Authorities declare that half the ship is prohibited territory from which the passengers must stay away because of a supposed outbreak of typhus. The passengers use a variety of methods to attempt to transgress the symbolic border that divides the two halves of the ship. The two halves, as well as the line that divides them, acquire allegorical value as the novel progresses. As the passengers attempt to enter the prohibited area, they seem to be striving to explore the "other" of their individual and collective lives. In this early novel, Cortázar begins his lifelong exploration of the role of chance, sexuality, and the absurd. Cortázar also begins to experiment with narrative techniques, juxtaposing several styles and types of wordplay.

In addition to several volumes of superb short stories, Cortázar wrote some interesting books that escape facile classification. His early and light *Cronopios and Famas* (1962) is a volume of highly inventive short vignettes about fantasy animals with entertainingly direct parallels to certain human types. *Around the Day in Eighty Worlds* (1967) is a collage of essays, drawings, and other creative pieces. In *Vampiros multinacionales* (Multinational vampires, 1975), he combines the comic-book form with political analysis, naming real people and events. By the mid-1970s, Cortázar was fully dedicated to the politics of writing and to writing about politics.

# Conclusion

With the possible exception of Borges, no Latin American writer has had more impact on Latin American fiction in recent decades than Cortázar. *Hopscotch* represented an epochal breakthrough for Latin American literature in the 1960s, as important as *Ficciones* had been in the 1940s. Latin American writing was not the same after Borges's seminal volume; the Latin American novel was not the same after *Hopscotch* either. Morelli's radical proposals for the novel opened the door for two generations of postmodern writing, represented by novels with direct precedents in *Hopscotch,* such as the Mexican José Emilio Pacheco's *You Will Die in a Distant Land* (1967) and the Colombian Alberto Duque López's *Mateo el flautista* (Mateo the flute player, 1968). Pacheco, Duque López, and a host of other young writers began to find new roles for the reader of fiction, just as Morelli had proposed.

Cortázar never had the broad, popular appeal of García Márquez and Vargas Llosa in the United States or Europe; he never published a "best-seller." A few of Cortázar's books fit more comfortably in the category of cult classics that have a small following of very devoted readers. In Latin America, he has been read more broadly, and his writings are deeply respected by the novelists of the Boom as well as by many other writers.

The other writers of the Boom have become more temperate and moderate in their politics since the 1970s and certainly less vocal in their defense of Fidel Castro. Cortázar, on the other hand, kept experimenting with ways of being a revolutionary writer, finding different methods in different stages of his career. Rarely did his fiction have anything significant to do with any specific political situation; rather, he conceived of his revolutionary role in terms far more abstract than any particular situation might involve. He invites his readers to question their uses of languages, their everyday behavior, and their mental habits. He agreed with Fuentes that the dualities of Western Manichaean thinking were far more insidious and limiting than any one political regime. Cortázar wrote in order to transform the way we read, write, and think, hoping to generate paradigm shifts that would radically change Western society.

# 10

# *The Novels of Mario Vargas Llosa*

Mario Vargas Llosa has been the enfant terrible of the Boom—its youngest and one of its most gifted storytellers, and the most politically out-of-step of them all over the past two decades. He was born in 1936, over two decades after Cortázar and almost a decade after Fuentes and García Márquez. Nevertheless, he has published a series of superb novels that have attracted a broad international readership as well as considerable scholarly attention. Since the early 1980s, he has been considered too conservative politically for the taste of much of Latin America's left. Vargas Llosa, in turn, has not been reticent to ridicule the left in essays and interviews.

Vargas Llosa burst onto the literary scene with his first novel, *The Time of the Hero*, in 1963. Before that, he had published some short stories in a volume titled *Los jefes* (1958) that was hardly noticed beyond a few friends in Peru; these stories appeared in English under the title *The Cubs and Other Stories*. He wrote them in the mid-1950s as a college student with great aspirations to be a writer in a country where being a full-time professional writer was an unheard-of proposition. Thanks to a literary prize that he won, however, he traveled to Europe (first Spain, then France) where he struggled to put together the literary career that skyrocketed after the publication of *The Time of the Hero*, which became an instant bestseller in Latin America. Always a disciplined professional, he has published over a dozen novels, as well as short fiction, literary criticism, essays, and plays. His major novels are *The Time of the Hero*, *The Green House* (1966), *Conversation in The Cathedral* (1969), and *The War of the End of the World* (1981).

## Major Novels

Vargas Llosa's fiction is of uniformly high quality. Although most critics tend to value his early novels the most highly, few doubt that the later *The War of the End of the World* was an unequivocal sign that his writing career had not ended in the 1960s. The early writing consists of three novels that Vargas Llosa has claimed helped free him from the "demons" of his childhood and adolescence in Peru (all the stories are set in his homeland). They are novels written in the Faulknerian mode—each one more complex in structure and use of dialogue, as well as narrative point of view. *The War of the End of the World,* on the other hand, is a masterpiece set not in Vargas Llosa's homeland, but in Brazil.

*The Time of the Hero,* a story about adolescents in a military school, has a narrative form structured with precision. It consists of 81 narrative segments that appear in two parts and an epilogue. Each of the two parts contains eight chapters, which generally consist of 4 or 5 narrative segments. One chapter has only one narrative segment, two chapters have 10 narrative segments, and the epilogue and three other chapters contain 3 narrative segments. This complex structure—which Vargas Llosa had learned from Faulkner—also features a variety of narrators within the story and outside the story. Approximately one-third of the novel—36 of the 81 segments—consists of first-person narrations.

The action that sets the novel in movement is the theft of a chemistry examination by Cava, a student in the Leoncio Prado Military School. Unable to identify the culprit, the school authorities confine all the cadets to the barracks indefinitely. After suffering confinement for several weeks and consequently unable to visit his girlfriend on the weekend, one of the cadets, nicknamed Slave (Ricardo Arana), reveals the thief's identity to the school officials in exchange for the right to leave the premises. The school subsequently expels Cava.

Jaguar, the aggressive leader of the cadets, along with his peers, suspects that someone has betrayed them. Soon thereafter, Slave is shot during some military maneuvers. Even though Jaguar appears to be guilty of the crime, the school officials conclude that the death is accidental, caused by Slave's own rifle. Slave's only friend, Alberto, is aware of the animosity Jaguar held toward Slave and tells the officials of the murder. Those in the upper echelon of the school hierarchy prefer to conceal the facts in order to prevent the scandal that would inevitably result. When school officials learn that Alberto had written pornographic stories to sell to his peers, they blackmail him into silence. The one officer who seems morally capable of questioning the situation, Gamboa, finds his career prospects ruined when he is sent to an isolated post in the provinces. An epilogue tells of the main characters' lives and careers after leaving the school.

The intricate plot development and the different temporal and spatial planes of reality make even an understanding of the novel's series of events and relationships among characters a challenging intellectual experience. As is always the case in Vargas Llosa's novels (and is not always the case in the fiction of Fuentes and Cortázar), suspense and plot development are essential. In *The Time of the Hero* two structures are developed in a parallel fashion. One involves a series of details related to character and plot; the second is the development of the novel in broader terms.

In the first half of the novel, a series of narrative segments appear regularly that are related by an unidentified youthful narrator. The fifth narrative segment of the first chapter is one such section: the reader experiences the sounds and words of the youth's perverse sexual acts, but the narrative filter is unidentified. This identity is only a minor issue because the reader's experience would not be radically altered by knowing who narrates. Nevertheless, as the novel progresses, the reader's curiosity is piqued. The question is answered at the beginning of the second half of the novel when the narrator identifies himself as Boa.

Similarly, the second narrative segment of the first chapter creates questions concerning identities when it describes the arrival of Richi or Ricardito to a new neighborhood, Magdalena Nueva. It soon becomes apparent that these narrative segments are describing Slave's childhood before he began attending the Leoncio Prado. By the third chapter, such flashback narratives dealing with Slave (and also Alberto) are no longer enigmatic; but another question surfaces: Who is the narrator of the first section, which deals with Tere and is related by a narrator within the story? The reader logically attempts to relate this section to Slave or perhaps even Alberto, since there are chapters associated with Tere during the novel's "present." Later, it will become apparent that these anecdotes, in fact, tell of Jaguar's relationship with Tere before his entrance into the Leoncio Prado.

These minor perplexities are an important factor in maintaining reader involvement in the first half of the novel. By the second half, most of these questions have been resolved and more thematic matters become central. The military exercise that ends part 1 is just a game of sorts, but a change takes place when Jaguar kills Slave: the potential death that terminates part 1 moves the novel to another plane of thematic importance. The problems of part 2 involve adults in real social contexts, not adolescent games. In the second half, moral issues become the substance of the novel. The central problem for the reader is how those involved will confront Slave's murder. If the reality of the adolescents in part 1 was one of instinctive cruelty and sordidness, the reality of the adults in part 2 is the calculated manipulation of human lives.

*The Time of the Hero* presents itself to the reader as a box of secrets. The minor and major questions involve both a moral questioning and a puzzle to be solved. The cadets' internal world is also one of secrets; it is one cadet's failure to keep a secret, after all, that is the main catalyst in the novel's action. In this way, Vargas Llosa develops a parallel between the cadets' secrets, structure, and the reader's experience: all are predicated on the issue of secrecy and solving the enigmas created by secrecy.

A significant factor in the reader's experience is the author's use of a variety of narrators. Twenty-six first-person narrations and the remaining third-person narrations are not uniform in their revelation of either the interior psychological realities of the characters or the presentation of exterior social reality. Critics of *The Time of the Hero* have correctly viewed its fictional world as a microcosm of Peruvian society. The novel portrays an unjust hierarchical society in which all social relations operate on the basis of dominance or coercion. The value of the text as a denunciation of certain characteristics of Peruvian and Latin American society, however, should not obscure the fact that the use of narrative point of view and other subjectifying factors are essential to the novel's total experience.

The structure and point of view in *The Time of the Hero* are effective vehicles for both creating the world of the Leoncio Prado Military School and inviting the reader to participate actively in this act of creation. Neither this type of structure nor use of point of view is, in itself, an innovation. Critics have already pointed out Vargas Llosa's technical predecessors, among them Dos Passos and Faulkner. At the end of this novel, however, the Peruvian writer pioneers a technique of telescoping time that he exploited more fully in his next two novels.[1]

Vargas Llosa has written an essay that the reader of *The Green House* can use to gain valuable insights into the personal experiences and Peruvian reality that, according to the author, were the basis for the creation of this novel. This essay, published in Spanish as *Historia secreta de una novela* (Secret history of a novel), explains many of the actual places, situations, and characters that appear in *The Green House*. Vargas Llosa begins his "secret history" by explaining the background to the two locations of the novel, Piura in northern Peru and Santa María de Nieva in the jungle. They represent two totally different historical, social, and geographical worlds. For the author, Piura represents civilization: it is the desert, the color yellow, cotton, and Spanish Peru. Santa María de Nieva is the jungle, vegetal exuberance, the color green, tribes that have not yet entered into the flow of Western history, and institutions and customs that seem to be left over from the Middle Ages and the Stone Age.

*The Green House* originated, according to this essay, in 1945, when the Vargas Llosa family arrived in Piura for the first time. Although they lived there for only a year, the writer claims that the things he did, and the people and places with which he became acquainted, remained so firmly imprinted in his memory that no other period in his life left such an impression.

The text of *The Green House* consists of four parts and an epilogue, each of which could be considered a prologue (although it is not identified as such in the text). Parts 1, 3, and the epilogue contain four chapters; parts 2 and 4 have three. The chapters of part 1 and 2 contain five narrative segments; those in parts 3 and 4 have four narrative segments. Numerous stories are woven through this novel, but the work offers two broad settings that correspond to two general plots. In the first setting, in Piura, a young man named Anselmo arrives and, after becoming well acquainted with Piura's inhabitants and ways of life, builds the Green House, a brothel, in the desert on the outskirts of the town. Despite the protests of Father García, the new establishment flourishes. Anselmo kidnaps a blind orphan girl, Antonia, and keeps her in the house, where he fathers a child whose birth causes Antonia's death. The outraged Father García and the women of Piura burn down the Green House. Eventually, a second Green House appears within the city that is owned by Chunga, Anselmo's daughter by Antonia. The old Anselmo regularly plays there in an orchestra. From the Mangachería, a group called the Champs, which includes Sergeant Lituma, frequents the Green House's bar. Lituma challenges a friend, Seminario, to a game of Russian roulette, and the latter's death results in Lituma's incarceration. Lituma's wife, Bonifacia, is seduced by one of the Champs and eventually works in the Green House as a prostitute.

The second setting and main plot, seemingly unrelated to the first, involves the story of indigenous tribes, merchants, government officials, and missionaries in the area of Santa María de Nieva in the Amazon. Government soldiers bring young Indian girls to the nuns for education at a mission in Santa María. The governor, Reátegui, operates a profitable business by trading for rubber and other goods at a very favorable rate of exchange and then selling the goods in the city of Iquitos. Reátegui tortures the Indian chief Jum for attempting to sell his own goods. A voice that narrates stories related to all these events is that of Fushía, who tells his friend Aquilino of all his operations and the key events of his life.

The logic of cause and effect in a sequential story line is systematically undermined in *The Green House*. Incidents leading to the development of conflicts as well as those pertaining to their resolution are revealed before the exposition of a climactic moment for each character. For example, Bonifacia's story involving the mission in Santa María de Nieva has not been fully developed when it is revealed that she has become a prostitute in Piura.

A complex pattern of relationships determines the reader's perception of the characters as human beings. They tend to lose their individual identities and exist, rather, as elements within the overall scheme. Crucial acts in the lives of the characters define them not so much in terms of their own personalities as in terms of their relationships to their surrounding world.

*The Green House* is a patently dialogic novel in ways more complex than even the theorist who invented the term—M. Bakhtin—probably could have imagined. First, the novel is richly dialogic in its incorporation of multiple layers by means of telescoping. The novel is also dialogic in its use of many-layered discourses from different spheres, such as religion and various social classes. The reader is in constant contact with a changing sense of the "real" in continual flux. Since the variant communications of languages are in opposition, reality takes on a capricious quality that the reader becomes accustomed to questioning. Reality becomes so innately relative, in fact, that the nature of truth and even the possibility of truth are called into question. And this type of questioning created by the techniques specific to *The Green House* is essential to the experience of the Vargas Llosa reader, who also comes to question the possibility of attaining a complete understanding exclusively through rational means.

Like Fuentes's *Terra Nostra* and García Márquez's *One Hundred Years of Solitude, Conversation in The Cathedral* also seems to be that impossible "total novel" much spoken about by Latin American writers and critics in the 1960s and 1970s. Vargas Llosa announces this "totalizing" project, this massive novel, with an epigram by Balzac. The author then goes on to portray the totality of fictionalized Peru as a corrupt and decadent nation.

A resounding question set forth by the protagonist in the second sentence of the novel reads as follows: "At what precise moment had Peru fucked itself up?" This question resonates and reappears throughout the text, and it can be associated with three of the novel's most fundamental characteristics. The first, suggested by the phrase "at what precise moment," points to the importance of time. Whereas in *The Green House* space takes priority over time, in *Conversation in The Cathedral* time takes priority over space. The second important element is Peru itself: the novel will be a portrayal and questioning of an entire nation during a specific historical period. Peru of the 1950s—under a dictatorship—is the subject of this book. The third significant characteristic is suggested by the question mark at the end of the sentence, because the novel presents itself initially as a question to be solved. The reader's task will involve attempting to solve a series of mysteries about character, plot and, indeed, what happened to Peru and when.

The novel actually begins in a "present" of the 1960s. The 32-year-old Santiago Zavala encounters Ambrosio Pardo, former chauffeur for Santiago's father, Fermín, and also for Cayo Bermúdez. Ambrosio is working at a dog pound where Santiago goes to claim his missing dog. They spend four hours in intense dialogue at a bar called The Cathedral. Their dialogue, in turn, is transmuted into other dialogues and anecdotes, which, in their totality, relate the story of their respective lives and those of many other individuals during the time from about 1948 to the early 1960s.

The complex and amorphous reality of *Conversation in The Cathedral* derives from a multiple set of narrative procedures. In the end, the reader may conclude that the complexity is a false one: nothing complex is happening, relatively simple events are being related as if they were a jigsaw puzzle. Before the reader will be able to reach such a conclusion, however, it will be necessary to experience a complex set of situations and even master a series of sophisticated narrative techniques.

The Peruvian society that the reader sees is devastating. The predominant image of the nation, already explored in *The Green House*, is that of Peru as a brothel. Don Cayo, the most powerful character in *Conversation in The Cathedral* , uses his entertainment privileges as a type of brothel, at the home of a character named Hortensia. A society that reduces human existence to such levels of debasement can make individuals as different as Santiago and Don Cayo surprisingly similar. By the end of the novel, both are reduced to total cynicism. The major characters live existences characterized primarily by frustration.

*Conversation in The Cathedral* is the apogee of the first period of Vargas Llosa's novelistic career. Like *The Time of the Hero* and *The Green House,* it deals with political and social realities—but on a larger scale than the two previous works. It is not predominantly a political novel, but a story of individual lives deeply affected by a particular political and social circumstance—a dictatorship. The reader's main concerns in part 4 of the novel, in fact, are not political events or characters, but the personal dramas of Santiago and Ambrosio, particularly as they relate to the persons around them: Fermín, Amalia, Ana, and Queta. The first chapter of part 3 is a melodramatic treatment of the death of Hortensia. This touch of melodrama is more fully developed in part 4: the potential history of a dictator proposed on the novel's first page ("At what precise moment had Peru fucked itself up?") has become in the end a narrative account of Santiago's marriage to the humble Ana, Ambrosio's problems in Pucallpa, and the like.

Its epic vision, apotheosis of storytelling, and fascinating characters are just three of several factors that make *The War of the End of the World* a synthesis of Vargas Llosa's writing career. It is a vast (some 568 pages) and challenging novel set in rural northeast Brazil near the end of the nineteenth century. Vargas Llosa retells the incredible story of an antigovernment rebellion by a community of religious fanatics and of the ensuing war between them and the equally fervent government soldiers. As is all too often the case with such "incredible" Latin American stories, the happenings in the Brazilian town of Canudos are based on actual historical events.

According to Vargas Llosa, he had never been as fascinated with a story as he had with the one involving Canudos.[2] His fabrication of history in novelistic form is the result of both chance and extensive research. Chance came into play when a Brazilian film director asked Vargas Llosa to write a filmscript for a movie using Canudos as a backdrop. Since the Peruvian knew nothing of the subject, he read *Rebellion in the Backlands* (1902) by Euclides Da Cunha, a classic book in Brazilian literature. Vargas Llosa then spent several months writing the script—but the picture was never made. Nevertheless, he decided to write the novel; it took four years of research in the Library of Congress and in Brazil.

*The War of the End of the World* consists of four parts, each of which contains between three and seven chapters. Most chapters contain four or five brief narrative segments, usually three to eight pages in length. Part 1 (120 pages) has seven chapters, each with four narrative segments. Part 2 (11 pages) contains only three brief chapters, with no divisions into narrative segments. Part 3 (209 pages) offers seven chapters, each with five narrative segments. Part 4 (215 pages) contains six chapters, each with four narrative segments. Although this structure may make the book appear similar in organization to *The Green House* or *Conversation in The Cathedral,* the novels are comparable in only the most superficial way; unlike the technically complex novels of the 1960s, *The War of the End of the World* is basically a straightforward narration related, for the most part, by a controlling omniscient narrator. In this sense, it is Vargas Llosa's most traditional novel.

Part 1 provides an introduction to most of the main characters and to the general historical and political setting. By the end of part 1, the religious fanatics of Canudos have stunned the government's soldiers by defeating the first two armies sent to the backlands to control them. The major characters introduced are Antonio Vicente Mendes Maciel (always called "the Counselor"), Galileo Gall, and Epaminondas Goncalves. The narrator presents the Counselor as a special and extraordinary individual, portraying him as a living legend and, by the end of part 1, even a Christlike figure.

Following the introduction of the characters on both sides and the intense military action in part 1—the two clashes between the inhabitants of Canudos and government soldiers—part 2 functions as a type of brief interlude. The reader is afforded the opportunity to be distanced from Canudos and view the situation as it is seen through the press in Bahia, in the state of Salvador.

Part 3, like the third act of a traditional four-act play, complicates the plot and intensifies the human drama. Two characters who will have enormous impact later on appear on the scene: Colonel Moreira César and the Baron of Canabrava. Moreira César arrives at the rural town of Queimadas as a hero of the Brazilian Republic. The Baron of Canabrava regards the military as a threat to the power of the landed aristocracy: a military victory in Canudos could precipitate a sweep into power. Concomitant with this political and military maneuvering, the fanatics in Canudos busy themselves with preparations to defend their town from the inevitable next attack.

Part 4 is dedicated almost entirely to the final siege of Canudos, which eventually destroys the fanatics and the remnants of the town. The first three chapters describe preparations for the siege and the beginning of the battle. The last three chapters, functioning as a type of epilogue, relate what has happened in Canudos after the battle.

As in Vargas Llosa's previous novels, plot in itself is once again a predominant factor. The difficult element for the reader of this novel is the density and length of the story rather than intercalated dialogues or complex relationships among fictional readers and writers. Narrative technique is in itself less of an explicit issue—and the effects of Vargas Llosa's techniques are more subtle—than in his more overtly Faulknerian texts.

Some of Vargas Llosa's constant thematic concerns reappear in *The War of the End of the World*. The fanaticism that emanates from both Canudos and some of the republicans has traces of the attitudes of characters in previous novels, such as Father García in *The Green House*. Once again, the novelist places in question the potential of the purely rational in comprehending reality. Rather than questioning reality by undermining it, as in *The Green House* and *Conversation in The Cathedral*, *The War of the End of the World* calls the rational into question by means of the characterization of Galileo Gall, who is one of the most intellectual and rational of Vargas Llosa's characters, as well as one of his most flagrant fools. The presence of the military, most evident before in *The Time of the Hero* and *Captain Pantoja and the Special Service,* is once again ushered forth as a central preoccupation. The fanaticism and rigidity of the military figures in *The War of the End of the World* make them victims, once again, of Vargas Llosa's critical and occasionally satirical pen. In addition, this novel brings forth broader issues, such as the conflict of ideologies, the conflict of individuals, and even a conflict of languages.

# Other Novels

Vargas Llosa's other novels are not as engaging as these; neverthe-less, they are obviously the fiction of a highly talented and mature writer. In the 1970s, he lightened his tone and published two humorous novels, *Captain Pantoja and the Special Service* (1973) and *Aunt Julia and the Script Writer* (1977). *Captain Pantoja and the Special Service* is a satire of the military, and *Aunt Julia and the Script Writer* is an entertaining work that combines autobiography and a parody of popular culture.

Since *The War of the End of the World,* Vargas Llosa has published novels dealing with different aspects of Peruvian reality, several of which have characters from his early fiction, such as Sergeant Lituma from *The Green House.* In *The Real Life of Alejandro Mayta* (1984), Vargas Llosa returns to a political situation in the increas-ingly violent Peru of the 1970s and 1980s. The key event in this novel is based on an 1958 armed rebellion in the village of Jauja in the Peruvian Andes. It is a 10-chapter novel that features a man named Mayta and a novelist as its main characters. The contempo-rary Peru of the narrator-novelist's "present" is a poor and strife-ridden nation seemingly headed toward chaos. In *The Storyteller* (1987), Vargas Llosa returns to the setting of the Peruvian jungle and to his traditional theme of the function of storytelling in society. Sergeant Lituma and some of Vargas Llosa's well-known thematic "demons" return in *Who Killed Palomino Molero?* (1986) and *Death in the Andes* (1993). He has also published a short novel that is an inventive dialogue with painting, *In Praise of the Stepmother* (1988).

# Conclusion

Vargas Llosa is a storyteller in the Faulknerian tradition that so per-vasively affected Latin America during the 1940s and 1950s; of the writers of the Boom, he and García Márquez were the most loyal to Faulkner in the early stages of their careers. This type of fiction, identified as transcendent regionalism in Spanish American litera-ture, has been practiced in a variety of ways since the rise of mod-ernist fiction in Latin America in the 1940s. Unlike Cortázar and some postmodern writers, Vargas Llosa has never questioned the value of storytelling in itself, but rather has sought to clarify in his fiction, essays, and plays how the writer creates and what function the story and storytelling have in society. *The Storyteller* is his most direct approach in fiction to this problem.

The writers of the Boom have all sought—using differing strategies—to be universal. Several characteristics of Vargas Llosa's themes and techniques contribute to his universality. The interest in the total novel noted in works such as *Conversation in The Cathedral* makes him comparable to such writers as Balzac, Tolstoy, and, once again, Faulkner. (This group would also include the Fuentes who conceived of his total work as a massive "La edad del tiempo" in 14 cycles.) The successful development and incorporation of literary romance—from the early stories through *The Green House* and *The War of the End of the World*—distinguishes Vargas Llosa from many Latin American writers who share his political and social perspectives but who produce a more overtly "social" literature. Most of Vargas Llosa's techniques, especially his use of dialogue, narrative point of view, and time, can be considered a particular and sometimes refined application of innovations originally heralded by Joyce, Dos Passos, and Faulkner. The structures and methods of narrative found in all his novels share in making the reader of Vargas Llosa an active participant in a continually direct, seemingly unmediated experience.[3]

# 11

# *The Novels of Gabriel García Márquez*

## Introduction

Master of magic realism, Nobel laureate, and the most consequential practitioner of the right of invention since Borges, Gabriel García Márquez has become virtually the emblem of modern Latin American literature in recent years, particularly in the United States and Europe. He is best known for his major work and, in particular, for one of the major novels written in the Spanish language since *Don Quixote, One Hundred Years of Solitude* (1967).

Son of a telegrapher, García Márquez was born in Aracataca, Colombia, in either 1927 or 1928.[1] Growing up in this small town in the northern Caribbean region of the country, he was reared by his grandparents and learned of the oral tradition that was still alive in the region from his grandmother, who he claims was an expert storyteller. From her, he heard the equivalent of the American tall tale at an early age. After attending high school near Bogotá and beginning his college studies there, he moved back to the Caribbean coast—Cartagena and then Barranquilla—in the late 1940s, where he practiced journalism, read the modernist masters, and began writing short stories. His idols were Faulkner and Hemingway. His early stories (ignored until he became a Nobel laureate) were amateurish attempts to fictionalize the subconscious, producing surrealist effects. His first novelistic project was a Faulknerian work titled *Leafstorm* (1955). In the mid-1950s, he went to Europe as a journalist and wrote the stories that later appeared as *Big Mama's Funeral* (1962), as well as the two short novels *No One Writes to the Colonel* (1961) and *In Evil Hour* (1962).

In these four works, García Márquez began creating his Macondo, the fictional world of his early work that is in some ways comparable to Faulkner's Yoknapatawpha County. After completing these books of fiction, García Márquez basically abandoned his career as a novelist, moving to Mexico in the early 1960s with the intention of dedicating himself strictly to another of his passions—film. In 1965, however, he spontaneously realized that he had one more novel to write. He isolated himself at home for a year in order to write the "complete" story of Macondo and to do so by using his original referent to storytelling—the oral narrative techniques of his grandmother. The result, of course, was that vast tale of Macondo told in an oral style, *One Hundred Years of Solitude*. Since it appeared, he has published numerous other books of fiction, as well as journalism.

# Major Novels

García Márquez's two major novels are the culmination of his cycle of Macondo, *One Hundred Years of Solitude* and the technical tour de force that he used to distance himself finally from Macondo, *The Autumn of the Patriarch*. Writers and critics hold several of his other works in high esteem, particulary *No One Writes to the Colonel* and *Love in the Time of Cholera* (1985).

*One Hundred Years of Solitude* is the story of the Buendía family and the story of Macondo. José Arcado Buendía marries his cousin, Ursula, both of whom are the first generation of a seven-generation family. Because of their kinship, José, Ursula, and all of their descendants live under the threat and terror of conceiving a child with a pig's tail. Macondo progresses from a primitive village to a modern town after the arrival of electricity, lights, and other twentieth-century conveniences. It also suffers the vicissitudes of Colombian (and Latin American) history, including civil wars.

This novel consists of 20 unnumbered and untitled chapters that tell the Macondo story in a basically linear fashion, with frequent but brief diversions into the past or future. The first 2 chapters provide the background of the family. The first focuses primarily on José Arcadio Buendía and the crazed methods he invents to attempt to understand the world. The second chapter moves back in the history of the family and describes the foundation of Macondo. It traces the family roots back to the sixteenth century, when Sir Francis Drake attacked the Colombian coastal region of Riohacha. One of the most remarked-upon episodes in chapter 3 depicts an insomnia plague that afflicts Macondo. With the insomnia comes a lack of memory. In the fourth chapter, the artist Pietro Crespi arrives in Macondo. In the chapters that follow, the novel moves into a rewriting of much of Colombia's history, including its numerous civil wars. The political situation seems to repeat itself in interminable cycles. A banana company from the United States arrives and refuses to give its workers decent wages, provoking a strike. Soldiers massacre thousands of strikers. After a lengthy rain, Macondo seems to be reborn. At the end of the novel, the family cycle is completed when a child is born with a pig's tail. Several references to literature itself—including writers of the Boom—create a sense of closure to the book.

*One Hundred Years of Solitude* might seem at first like a book of fantasy, but it is one of the most historical books of the Boom and it abounds in social and political implications. Colonel Aureliano Buendía, who fights endless battles in the novel, is modeled after a late-nineteenth-century figure, General Rafael Uribe Uribe, who was a leader of the liberals who suffered numerous defeats in Colombia. The strike of the banana workers, which is related as one of the most fantastic events in the novel, is, in fact, one of the most historical episodes. In November 1928, Colombian workers declared a strike against the United Fruit Company. García Márquez was among the first to relate this black period in the country's history, which resulted in the massacre of several hundred workers.

The narrator in *One Hundred Years of Solitude* is third-person omniscient, occasionally revealing what the characters think. The predominant mode, however, is external: the reader observes the characters act and speak. In most of the novel, this detached narrator offers seemingly neutral observations about the fictional world. Despite the omniscience and detachment, however, the narrator also functions as if he were a character in the novel. At times, he demonstrates an innocence or amazement with the world similar to that of the characters. The narrator thinks like the people of Macondo, at times demonstrating the same prejudices, at others the same primitiveness.

One consistently used technique of oral storytelling that García Márquez probably learned from his grandmother is an absolute coolness or understatement when describing incredible situations, and overstatement or exaggeration when dealing with the commonplace. In an episode concerning ice in the first chapter, the narrator employs these strategies. Initially, the narrator's language shares the characters' exaggerated reaction to the ice—it is described as the "largest diamond in the world." By the end of the episode, the narrator uses words such as *mysterious* and *prodigious* to describe what would seem to readers the most commonplace of everyday experiences, touching ice.

In contrast, the narrator regularly reacts to the most marvelous and fantastic things with absolute passivity—the lesson in technique García Marquez learned from his grandmother. In the first chapter, José and his children experience the disappearance of a man who becomes invisible after drinking a special potion. Neither the narrator nor the characters pay particular attention to this incredible occurrence.

There are only rare exceptions to the narrator's third-person omniscience. The entire issue of the narrator undergoes a radical change at the end of the novel when it is revealed that in reality the narrator of the entire story was a gypsy, Melquíades, who had appeared in the first chapter. Suddenly the reader comes to the realization that the narrator is not outside the story but within. This discovery underscores the story's basic fictionality, another technique that might have been momentarily forgotten by the reader absorbed in this history of Colombia and Western civilization. Another exception to the narrator's basic third-person omniscience occurs in chapter 16 when Fernanda creates an extensive monologue.[2]

Walter Ong has observed that many cultures and subcultures, even with a high-technology ambiance, preserve much of their original and primary orality.[3] García Márquez, a sophisticated product of a writing culture, juxtaposes print culture with much of the residually oral milieu of his youth in Aracataca. Both a primary oral culture and a sophisticated writing culture permeate *One Hundred Years of Solitude,* often in hilarious juxtaposition. Much of this novel recreates precisely the shift from orality to writing, changes hitherto labeled as shifts from "magic" to "science," which can be more cogently explained as shifts from orality to various stages of literacy.

This transition from orality to various stages of literacy is essential to the experience of *One Hundred Years of Solitude* and is particularly evident when one compares the initial chapters with the ending. In the first chapter, the mind-set of a primary orality predominates; in the last chapter, the most intricate exercises of a writing culture are carried out. In the first chapter, these two extremes are represented by Melquíades, who is of a writing culture from the outside, and by

Ursula, who possesses a mind-set of orality. The Macondo of the first paragraph is a place of paradisaical and primary orality in which stones are "white and enormous, like prehistoric eggs." The word *prehistoric* associates Macondo with a prehistory, prewriting stage. It is not only a prewriting stage but also one that borders on prespeaking. José Arcadio Buendía, between the two extremes of Melquíades and Ursula, serves as a special link in this chapter between oral and writing cultures. He also paradoxically belongs to both, reacting in some circumstances as an oral-culture person and in others as the only writing person in the predominantly oral milieu. Although José Arcadio Buendía is literate, he reacts to science with the same ingenuousness of an oral person, conceiving of Melquíades's magnets, for example, as a "weapon of war." Also typical of an oral-culture person's reaction to a writing mind-set is José Arcadio Buendía's response to Melquíades: he believes that Melquíades's knowledge had reached "unbearable" extremes. Oral-culture persons tend to view many of the modes and concerns of a writing culture as irrelevant or even ridiculous. Similarly, Ursula, in the first chapter, is uninterested in definitions and loses her patience with José Arcadio Buendía when he defines the world as round like an orange. The oral mind-set is also situational rather than abstract, the former being Ursula's constant mode of operation. When José Arcadio Buendía attempts to convince her to move from Macondo with his (abstract) fantastic stories and the (abstract) promise of a prodigious world, her response is to bring him down from this high level of abstraction to the concrete reality of the present, admonishing him to think less about crazy inventions and more about taking care of his sons. Thus, the first chapter emerges as an orality (Ursula), a writing culture (Melquíades), and a humorous semiorality (José Arcadio Buendía) that bridges the gap between the two.

After the first chapter, Macondo moves from preliteracy to literacy. The narrator's mind-set also shifts from the feigned preorality of the first chapter to the historicity of the second. In the first chapter, he had used the preliteracy image of prehistoric eggs; in the first line of the second chapter, he uses the historical discourse of writing—"When the pirate Sir Francis Drake attacked Riohacha in the sixteenth century, Ursula Iguarán's great-great-grandmother became so frightened with the ringing of alarm bells and the firing of cannons that she lost control of her nerves and sat down on a lighted stove."[4] In the final chapters, *One Hundred Years of Solitude* announces itself not only as writing but also as an example of the highly sophisticated forms of self-conscious fiction. It incorporates characters from other contemporary fictions and García Márquez's literary friends and characterizes Aureliano as reader in the act of deciphering parchments, which tell the story the reader has been reading.

*One Hundred Years of Solitude* contains several other qualities typical of oral-noetic processes. One of these, also typical of the tall tale, is the use of "heavy characters," persons whose deeds are monumental, memorable, and commonly public. The extensive litany of José Arcadio Buendía's exploits after his return from 65 trips around the world (chapter 5) and Colonel Aureliano Buendía's military exploits (including losing 32 battles) are perhaps the best example of this particular noetic process. Another typical oral process, already alluded to in the case of Ursula, is the use of concepts in situational frames of reference that are minimally abstract in the sense that they remain close to the human lifeworld. The narrator assumes this role as an oral-culture person throughout much of the novel, often using down-to-earth and animal imagery, thus remaining close to the human lifeworld.

What has often been identified in this novel by the now overused and frequently vague term "magic realism" can be more precisely described as a written expression of the shift from orality to various states of literacy. The effects of the interplay between oral and writing culture are multiple. García Márquez has fictionalized numerous aspects of his youth in the oral culture of rural Aracataca in Colombia. The unique traditionalism and modernity of this novel are based on various roles the narrator assumes as oral storyteller in the fashion of the tall tale, as narrator with an oral person's mindset, and as the modern narrator of a self-conscious (written) fiction. *One Hundred Years of Solitude* is a culmination of García Márquez's cycle of Macondo as well as a synthesis of oral and writing traditions extant in the northern Caribbean region of Colombia.

*The Autumn of the Patriarch* is García Márquez's novel of a dictator. In the late 1960s and early 1970s, the writers of the Boom had considered the possibility of writing a joint project about the archetypal Latin American dictator. They never did carry out the project together, but several Latin American writers did, in fact, publish novels about dictators. After a hiatus of eight years since publishing *One Hundred Years of Solitude* (a period in which he published journalism and a few stories), García Márquez came forth with his novel based on several dictators in Latin America. All of his works are well crafted; this novel is his most refined project of technical virtuosity.

García Márquez had begun this project at the end of Pérez Jiménez's dictatorship in Venezuela during the 1950s. Upon arriving in Caracas from Europe in 1958, García Márquez witnessed the downfall of Pérez Jiménez and the spectacle created by the nation-wide celebration. The figure of Pérez Jiménez, nevertheless, was merely a point of departure. García Márquez also began reading histories of dictators, books containing anecdotes that can make the most fantastic Latin American fiction read like stodgy realism. For example, García Márquez told of reading about a recent Haitian dictator, Duvalier, who ordered all black dogs in the country killed because he was convinced one of his political enemies had transformed himself into a black dog. García Márquez himself has explained that his intention in writing *The Autumn of the Patriarch* was to create a synthesis of all the Latin American dictators, but especially those from the Caribbean, including Venezuela.[5]

The protagonist of *The Autumn of the Patriarch* is a dictator, and the setting is an unnamed nation located vaguely in the Caribbean. The novel's main theme is power; from the days of the Pérez Jiménez dictatorship, García Márquez was intrigued by what he called the "mystery of power."[6]

The first chapter begins with the discovery of the rotting corpse of the protagonist (the General) in his presidential palace. The narrative moves quickly to several anecdotes about his life. The central anecdote in this chapter is what is identified as his "first death," that of his government-appointed double, Patricio Aragonés. The action of the second chapter is centered on the woman with whom the General falls obsessively in love, Manuela Sánchez. The third chapter deals with the politics of power. His power seems limitless: he is capable of changing the weather and signaling with his finger so that trees give fruit, animals grow, and men prosper. The General's power begins to wane in the fourth chapter, and his ability to understand either his loss of power or a diminishing contact with reality seems limited. The last two chapters narrate his final demise. The General marries Nazareno Leticia and has a child with her. The wife and child are assassinated, and dogs rip apart their corpses in a public plaza. The General hires a smooth and handsome henchman, Sáenz de la Barra, to carry out the sadistic assassinations he feels the government needs. The supreme dictator celebrates his one-hundredth anniversary in power, but thereafter his reign is decadent in every sense of the word. He dies unsure of the power that he exercised and by which he was tormented in the solitude of his dictatorship.

Throughout this novel, a fundamental technique in characterizing the General and developing the themes is the contrast between interior and exterior views of the novelistic world. In contrast to the godlike power that the General manipulates both among the citizenry and in his own self-estimation, a view of his psyche consistently emphasizes his pettiness and puerility. Throughout the novel, the General carefully and repetitively locks an elaborate combination of three crossbars, three locks, and three bolts in his room, thus underlining his paranoia. Despite his godlike self-confidence, the only person "authorized" to defeat him in a game of dominoes is his friend Rodrigo de Aguilar.

The technique of contrasting the exterior and interior views of the General is particularly effective in passages in which the focus changes from the exterior to the interior within sentences. For example, an attempted assassination is foiled by the General when he confronts the potential assassin holding him at gunpoint and screams: "I dare you, you bastard, I dare you." When the assassin hesitates, the General attacks him, calls his guards, and orders the victim tortured. After the narration of this anecdote by an omniscient narrator (with occasional interjections by the General), the story is completed at the very end of the final sentence by a shift to the interior focus (of which those who saw him were not aware): "He disappeared into the hearing room like a fugitive lightning flash toward the private quarters, he went into the bedroom, shut the three crossbars, the three bolts, the three locks, and with his fingertips he took off the pants he was wearing that were soaked in shit."[7] Until the narrator reveals the General's reactions in the last three words, the reader's view has been exterior and similar to that of the people observing the General's reactions. The last three words provide a contrasting interior characterization of the General, thus creating the humor.

In *The Autumn of the Patriarch*, García Márquez presents the maintenance of power as the result of the General's ability to manipulate the visible and the invisible. After the assassination attempt fails, the General not only orders the man put to death but also—more significantly in the context of his own understanding of the importance of the visible—orders that different parts of the assassin's body be exhibited throughout the country, thus providing a visible manifestation of the consequences of questioning his power. When he feels the necessity to exert maximum control of his power, he visibly observes its functioning. This need also explains the General's bizarre insistence in observing the milking of the cows each morning.

The question of the visible and the invisible and its relation to the novel's main theme, power, is also elaborated through the presence of the sea (mar) in the novel. As the predominant visible object in the General's daily life, the sea is his most treasured possession. The General's sea, his window, and his power become so intimately associated that he insists upon maintaining possession of his window and his sea as persistently as he does with maintaining his power. When he is in the process of losing his power, he is adamant about not losing his sea. The opening of a seen reality into a confluence of the visible and the invisible makes the experience of the novel similar to the principal theme it develops: the illusion of reality and power. Although the cycle of novels focused on Macondo is complete with *The Autumn of the Patriarch,* the universal experience created in it is a continuation of the transcendent regionalism so evident in García Márquez's previous work, especially *One Hundred Years of Solitude.*

# Other Novels

García Márquez had published some outstanding novels before *One Hundred Years of Solitude* and has also written several since *The Autumn of the Patriarch. Leafstorm* (1955), *No One Writes to the Colonel* (1961), and *In Evil Hour* (1962) were the novels of the cycle of Macondo that were, in effect, the smaller pieces that led up to his 1967 masterpiece. *Leafstorm* was written when García Márquez was clearly an admirer of Faulkner, and it reads much like *As I Lay Dying.* Most of the action takes place from 1903 to 1928 and the story is of Macondo. The focus is primarily on four characters: three persons in a family who narrate and a doctor whose wake is the basic circumstance of the novel. The first of these narrators is a ten-year-old boy who, at his father's wake, relates his thoughts and perceptions of the moment. The other narrative voices are the boy's mother, Isabel, and his grandfather. *No One Writes to the Colonel* is a book of silence; the silence is the work of an articulated and also a nonarticulated political censorship. The book's protagonist, an aged colonel, as well as Macondo's other inhabitants, avoid political language at all costs. The political situation is the essential and overriding factor in everyone's life. Consequently, this minimalized political discourse, resulting in a discourse of silence, is the novel's outstanding feature. *In Evil Hour* deals with the same basic political situation, but the presentation is more direct; violence and other physical acts are visible. Subversion and repression are not the nonarticulated taboo subjects of clandestine newspapers or conversations, but the central actions of the novel, which tells the story of life in an unnamed town (Macondo) during 17 days from the fourth of October to the twenty-first.

Since the publication of *The Autumn of the Patriarch* in 1975, García Márquez has written numerous books of fiction and nonfiction; his most notable novels have been *Chronicle of a Death Foretold* (1981) and *Love in the Time of Cholera* (1985). *Chronicle of a Death Foretold* is based on a 1951 newspaper story involving honor and death in Colombia. García Márquez's work is a kind of mystery novel in reverse, since the reader knows from the first line that the protagonist will be killed. The reader's only task is to discover exactly *how* the death will happen. The circumstances surrounding the death of the protagonist, Santiago Nassar, become increasingly more incredible: everyone in the town except Santiago himself knows he is going to die, yet no one says anything. The narrative provides no underlying system leading to a profound and coherent understanding of things. Rather, as in all of García Márquez's work, life is determined by inexplicable forces and irrational acts.

*Love in the Time of Cholera* is a novel about romance and aging. The elderly protagonist, Florentino Ariza, writes love letters to Fermina Daza for years, creating a love affair that is perhaps more a literary act than anything else. This novel contains many of the stylistic traits associated with the García Márquez of *One Hundred Years of Solitude,* as well as characters who are—in the mid-1980s—clichés of various characters in his earlier novels. Once again, the female characters are intuitive and stable, while the males are not. A lengthy and entertaining story, *Love in the Time of Cholera* can also be read as a parody of García Márquez's own writing of the Macondo period.

# Conclusion

When García Márquez became in 1982 the first writer of the Boom to receive the Nobel Prize for literature, it was the most prestigious recognition possible for one of the major writers of the century and the Latin American writer who most convincingly reaffirmed the right of invention in the Spanish language since Borges. Since his work had already been translated and lauded throughout the world before the decision of the Nobel judges, the prize was an effect and not a cause; García Márquez's writing over the previous three decades spoke for itself.

Like the other writers of the Boom—and particularly Cortázar—García Márquez prefers to see his creation as a revolutionary project. Social critic in his fiction and assertively leftist in his public political stances, García Márquez, nevertheless, has never been doctrinaire in his fiction writing. His ability to capture so much of Hispanic culture and history at the same time that he expresses so much of his participation in humanity in a universally appreciated way is one magnificent characteristic of his work. In this sense it is possible to understand García Márquez's own contention that the revolutionary role of the novelist is to "write well."

# 12

# *Inside and Outside the Boom*

## Introduction

The rise of the Boom, the appearance of Borges in translation in 1962, and the awarding of the Nobel Prize in literature to Miguel Angel Asturias in 1967 brought Latin American literature to a broad and enthusiastic international readership for the first time in history. The novelists of the Boom, as well as many other Latin American authors, benefited enormously from the fact that the region's writing was in the limelight. Nevertheless, many other fine novelists were seemingly overlooked, in some cases because of the attention given to the writers of the Boom. The Chilean José Donoso, the Brazilians Clarice Lispector and João Guimarães Rosa, and the Venezuelan Salvador Garmendia, among others, can be read (or reread) in this light.

By the 1960s, the Latin American novel obviously was a mature artistic form, and it had numerous masters besides García Márquez, Fuentes, Vargas Llosa, and Cortázar. The Chilean José Donoso published an impressive set of novels and, as a personal friend of these writers, was sometimes associated with the Boom. He probably never gained the renown of the others because he never published an international best-seller and he did not speak with a strong political voice in Latin America. The Venezuelan Salvador Garmendia was perhaps the exemplary novelist not part of the Boom: he has written a long and uninterrupted series of novels and short stories since the 1960s but has remained basically ignored by critics and the international readership outside of Venezuela. Rarely has he even traveled outside of Venezuela. The Brazilians Clarice Lispector and João Guimarães Rosa have fared little better, although they have been translated amply into Spanish and a little into English.

Novelists such as Donoso, Lispector, and Garmendia write a type of fiction that differs markedly from the major fictions of the Boom.

These novelists generally do not write the works of expansive geo-graphies and histories observed during the Boom—for example, *The Green House* or *One Hundred Years of Solitude*. Their work has none of the magic realism or broad historical vision of García Márquez. Their lack of a broad readership could well have less to do with the quality of their writing than with their lack of interest in fictionaliz-ing those elements of Latin American culture that most appeal to foreign readers.

# José Donoso

José Donoso has been the major novelist in Chile since the 1960s, and many scholars consider him the principal Chilean novelist of the century. From an upper-class family in Chile and educated at Princeton University, he dedicated a lifetime to fiction writing, pro-ducing well over a dozen books of fiction before his death in 1996. His early fiction dates back to the 1950s, but his reputation grew with the rise of the Boom (with which he was associated) and with the publication of his voluminous and hermetic novel *The Obscene Bird of the Night* in 1970. A close personal friend of Fuentes and occa-sional collaborator with the other writers of the Boom, he socialized with them and wrote a memoir about his experiences, *The Boom in Spanish-American Literature: A Personal History* (1972).

*The Obscene Bird of the Night* is Donoso's experiment in subverting the tenets of the traditional novel that were still dominant in Chile in the 1960s. Indeed, it is a lengthy catalogue of the narrative strata-gems associated with modernist fiction and could also be seen as one of those works of the Boom, like *Hopscotch*, that affected the later production of postmodern fiction in Latin America. Much of this highly fragmented work consists of the monologue of charac-ters in a constant process of transformation, most prominently Humberto Peñaloza and Mudito. Much of the novel takes place on an estate owned by an aristocratic couple, Jerónimo and Inés de Azcoitía, which seems to be populated by as many monsters and ghostlike marginal beings as by recognizable human characters. Rather than developing a story line, the novel is a work of multiple threads of voices, characters, and actions over which an author fig-ure occasionally presides. To some extent, it is a novel about politi-cal and economic power; and Donoso is equally concerned about the authority of the author figure, for this work is also a self-conscious fiction.

Donoso's earlier novels, *Coronation* (1957), *Hell Has No Limits* (1966), and *This Sunday* (1966), were more closely associated with realism and Donoso's interests in exploring interior, psychological spaces than they were with the right of invention, the other writings of the Boom, or the radical experimentation of *The Obscene Bird of the Night*. Most of his main characters are aristocrats; Donoso's family belonged to this privileged class in Chile. *Coronation* is a novel of decadence; the general setting of this early work is the large estates of an upper class that has lost its legitimacy. The emerging working classes begin to enter and interfere with the world of the wealthy and idle bourgeoisie. The basic plot deals with the attraction that an upper-class gentleman feels toward his servant, a relationship that threatens the stability of class differences. In *Hell Has No Limits*, a small rural town is a symbolic hell where the arrival of a transvestite performer destabilizes local relations. *This Sunday* is a return to the problems of the old aristocracy and class differences in Chile. In it, Donoso is once again concerned with the subtleties of human relations and the role of class, as well as the intangible ways in which the human psyche can affect human relations.

Donoso's fiction after *The Obscene Bird of the Night* includes several volumes of fiction and novels, but none are as ambitious and hermetic as that work. *A House in the Country* appears—on the surface—to be yet another novel about an oligarchic and decadent family, but it is an allegory of the Chilean military coup of 1973. Donoso's later work, such as *The Garden Next Door* (1981), has become more self-conscious and postmodern. For many readers and some scholars, he was basically a participant in the Boom.

# Clarice Lispector

Greatly admired among Latin American writers and a major twentieth-century Brazilian writer, Clarice Lispector, nevertheless, was never associated with the Boom. Before her death in 1977, she published over 20 books of fiction, including some superb short stories equal in quality to those of Borges and Cortázar. Her daring narrative experiments began to gain international attention in the early 1960s, and her work has been amply translated into numerous languages.

Like Donoso, her fiction is at the opposite end of the spectrum from magic realism; rather than the broad historical vision of Fuentes and García Márquez, she wrote "small-screen" novels of human relationships.[1]

Lispector's major books of fiction are *Family Ties* (1960), *The Apple in the Dark* (1967), and *The Hour of the Star* (1977). *Family Ties* is more a volume of well-honed short stories than a novel and deals with the everyday drama of human relations. In *The Apple in the Dark* (1967), she continues her in-depth analysis of the subtleties of human relations. *The Hour of the Star* deals with a young woman who leaves behind a life of poverty in northeastern Brazil in order to seek success in the city. This basic plot, of course, could be that of many nineteenth-century Latin American novels. A special relationship between the narrator and the young woman, however, distances this novel from those works. In the end, the narrator's particular role evokes the theme of identity as much as it illuminates the protagonist's social and economic plight.

# João Guimarães Rosa

Author of one stunning novel and several exceptionally impressive volumes of short stories, João Guimarães Rosa is generally recognized as one of the major novelists of the century in Brazil. Indeed, his lengthy, dense, and labyrinthine novel *The Devil to Pay in the Backlands* (1956) is considered by many scholars to be one of the monumental Latin American novels of the century—comparable to Cortázar's *Hopscotch* and Fuentes's *Terra Nostra*. Nevertheless, Guimarães Rosa died in 1967 as a writer highly respected by other writers and scholars but relatively unknown by the general reading public outside of Brazil. As a writer much admired by later generations, he left his mark on some of the postmodern fiction of the 1970s and 1980s.

*The Devil to Pay in the Backlands* is a 600-page monologue with no chapter divisions. Set in the Brazilian hinterland, this experimental and hermetic novel deals with a fictional interlocutor who spends three days listening to Riobaldo, an old gunslinging cowboy, tell stories of his life. There is no basic story line with any sense of chronological order. Rather, the anecdotes unfold on the basis of association, with one story or incident triggering another. The anecdotes deal with violent conflicts among rival groups in the rural area, while at another level of reading, there are several suggestions of a pact between the narrator and the devil. The reader is invited to analyze and judge the narrator, both because of the ambiguous relationship with the devil and an equally ambiguous relationship—with sexual overtones—with another bandit.

This novel can be associated with the special regionalism—transcendent regionalism—that was practiced in Latin America from the generation of Asturias to that of García Márquez. Guimarães Rosa's transcendent regionalist mode, however, is far less accessible than is that of Asturias, García Márquez, or even Vargas Llosa. This Brazilian practices the right of invention in his experimentation with language more freely than any of these others. Even the native speaker of Portuguese finds *The Devil to Pay in the Backlands* problematic to read because some of the language—as much as it sounds like Portuguese—is actually invented. The language of this novel can be described as baroque because of the frequent use of a precious literary vocabulary, invented syntactic constructions, Latinisms, agglutinations, expletives, and even words from Indian languages.

Given all the complexities involved with reading this epic work, it is a novel that, like Joyce's *Ulysses* and Fuentes's *Terra Nostra,* scholars have gradually unraveled and interpreted after many readings over several years. The quest motif is central to the novel and is similar to the quest motif as it has been developed in a variety of Western and Eastern literature.

Guimarães Rosa's several volumes of short stories, published from the 1940s to the 1960s, are generally as inventive and hermetic as his novel. Many of them are so experimental and lengthy that they barely fit any classification into the genre of the short story. Along with *The Devil to Pay in the Backlands,* they represent writings of one of Latin America's most accomplished fiction writers.

# Salvador Garmendia

Belonging to the same generation as writers of the Boom and as productive as the writers of the past three decades, Garmendia has, nevertheless, been virtually ignored outside of Venezuela. He has published over 15 books of fiction since the late 1950s, beginning with *Los pequeños seres* (1959, The little beings).

Garmendia and several other Venezuelan writers in the 1960s formed a group called Sardio; like the writers of the Boom, they wanted to modernize and urbanize literature. In *Los pequeños seres*, Garmendia represents these interests well, as he uses modernist narrative strategies in a novel set in an urban locale. As such, Garmendia's first novel, portraying an anguished office worker, is a landmark work in Venezuela. Garmendia's next novels, *Los habitantes* (1961, The inhabitants) and *Día de ceniza* (1964, Day of ashes), follow along the thematic and technical lines established in his first novel. *Los habitantes* is a psychological portrayal of an unemployed truck driver. The main character of *Día de ceniza* is a frustrated writer. *La mala vida* (1968, The bad life) is another portrayal of an anguished protagonist, this one living between the past and the present.

Garmendia, like Donoso and Lispector, is a small-screen novelist who is a master of narrative technique. In the early 1960s, he was in the avant-garde among a small group of Latin American writers— including Fuentes—who were successfully using the narrative strategies recently pioneered by the French in the *nouveau roman*. In addition, Garmendia has used techniques appropriated from film.

## Other Novelists

In addition to Donoso, Lispector, Guimarães Rosa, and Garmendia, several other accomplished Latin American writers published novels in the 1960s without receiving the international recognition of the writers of the Boom. They generally wrote fiction in the modernist vein, but without the flashiness of Fuentes or Cortázar and free of the exoticism of García Márquez or Vargas Llosa. The Cubans Guillermo Cabrera Infante and José Lezama Lima, the Mexican Rosario Castellanos, the Colombian Manuel Mejía Vallejo, and the Paraguayan Augusto Roa Bastos all fit in this category.

Cabrera Infante began writing in Cuba, then went into exile in the 1960s. He has published a continual flow of books since then, most of which escape easy genre definition. His major work—the novel of most impact—is *Three Trapped Tigers* (1967), a disperse and witty book set in prerevolutionary Cuba. After a prologuelike opening set in a Havana nightclub, the novel is narrated by three characters who take us through a zany world that seems to be nearing an end. As such, the predominant tone is one of nostalgia. Cabrera Infante is wildly experimental with language and, in this sense, is a pioneer in Latin America, with only two notable Joycean predecessors— Guimarães Rosa and Cortázar. His general practice of the right of invention with language, his constant wordplay, and his use of neologisms make *Three Trapped Tigers* an important predecessor of the postmodern novel in Latin America.

José Lezama Lima was best known for his lengthy career as a poet, but his novel *Paradiso* (1966) was a major work of the 1960s that was written about by Fuentes, Vargas Llosa, and Cortázar soon after its publication. It is the story of José Cemí, but the dense language and digressive style make any clear sense of plot questionable. Its language is intensely metaphorical, justifying Lezama Lima's own description of it as a "poem-novel."[2] As he develops both the time-bound story of the Cemí family and the time-free elements of metaphorical language, Lezama Lima confronts the contradictions of time and language throughout this text.[3] Neither the chapters of *Paradiso* nor its characters are linked to a particular time frame. Rather, the characters themselves are metaphors who are in constant search of origins, a search that is the primary theme of the novel. The year after Lezama Lima's death in 1976, his second novel, *Oppiano Licario*, appeared in print. This novel continues the story of José Cemí and his attempt to transcend the limits of everyday existence. As in *The Devil to Pay in the Backlands,* an underlying theme in both of Lezama Lima's works is the quest.

A prominent fiction writer, poet, and essayist in Mexico, Rosario Castellanos, unlike Donoso and Lezama Lima, was basically ignored by the writers of the Boom. Nevertheless, she did publish 27 books before her death in 1974. If it were not for her relatively sparse novelistic production in the 1960s and her premature death, she would have been the prime candidate to be the female voice of the Boom. Her recognition beyond Mexico came late, but it finally arrived in the form of scholarly attention in the 1970s and 1980s as well as with the publication of the *Rosario Castellanos Reader* in English in 1988.

Castellanos is a writer associated with feminism and the Indian world in which she grew up—Chiapas, Mexico. Her first novel, *Balún Canán* (1957), appeared in English in 1959 as *The Nine Guardians*. In this first work, she novelizes the Mesoamerican cosmogony. Her major novel, *Oficio de tinieblas* (1962, The dark service), was based on a historical uprising of the Chamula Indians in Chiapas in 1867 and had a unique protagonist for a Latin American novel: a female Indian. Although Castellanos was not as interested in language per se as Lezama Lima or Guimarães Rosa, *Oficio de tinieblas* exhibits a mastery of narrative technique comparable to the best craftsmanship seen during the Boom.

Manuel Mejía Vallejo, like Garmendia and Castellanos, has been the antithesis of the jet-set public intellectual associated with the Boom. He has spent his lifetime writing in his farmhouse in rural Antioquia, Colombia, rarely traveling beyond nearby Medellín, much less abroad. His writing career began in the late 1940s and has continued unabated into the 1990s. He has published over 20 books of fiction, his major novels being *El día señalado* (1964, The special day) and *Aire de tango* (1975, Air of tango). *El día señalado* is a novel dealing with political violence in Colombia in the 1950s written in a way that incorporates both oral tradition and the aesthetics of modernism. *Aire de tango* is Mejía Vallejo's homage to the Argentine tango. Set in a tango bar in a working-class neighborhood of Medellín, this novel reveals one little-known aspect about this Colombian city (often more associated today with drugs): its citizens are as enthusiastic about the Argentine tango as are many of the most dedicated tango lovers in Buenos Aires and Paris.

The Paraguayan Augusto Roa Bastos has spent much of his life in exile in France and, consequently, has enjoyed much more public visibility in Europe and Latin America than Mejía Vallejo, Garmendia, or Castellanos. He has written over 20 books of fiction, essays, and poetry, although he is best known for his landmark novel *Yo, el Supremo* (1974, I, the Supreme), which is in the vein of the dictator novels that several novelists of the Boom published in the 1970s. The other works of this type, such as García Márquez's *The Autumn of the Patriarch*, fictionalized these dictators by synthesizing several historical figures. Roa Bastos, on the other hand, based his novel closely on the life and career of one Paraguayan dictator, José Gaspar Francia, who ruled Paraguay from 1914 to 1940. The first-person narrator presents himself simultaneously as historian and playful intervenor in the text. Several other voices also enter to make this apparently modernist project of historical revisionism, in reality, more a postmodern reflection on language and writing.

# Conclusion

A few of the writers never recognized as part of the select group of the Boom, nevertheless, occupied ambiguous positions inside and outside its parameters. Donoso, Cabrera Infante, and Lezama Lima, to varying degrees, participated in the Boom, interacted with its members in the private and public sphere, and perhaps even benefited, albeit in minor ways, from the rise of the Boom as a cultural phenomenon in Latin America. In some ways, each of these three writers managed to assume some role as the public intellectual, a role in which Fuentes, Vargas Llosa, and García Márquez excelled in the 1960s and 1970s. Roa Bastos has also been active in the public sphere of politics.

On the other hand, numerous gifted writers in Latin America were either unable or unwilling to assume such a public identity; Lispector, Guimarães Rosa, Mejía Vallejo, and Castellanos exemplify that category. The list of talented and productive writers in Latin America whose work has passed by with far less recognition than it deserves stretches far beyond the authors presented here; a more complete catalogue would include, for example, the Argentinian David Viñas and the Mexican Sergio Galindo.

Some talented writers simply do not write for a readership as broad as did the writers of the Boom. Hermetic novels such as Guimarães Rosa's *The Devil to Pay in the Backlands* and Lezama Lima's *Paradiso* are not destined to become best-sellers, and their authors did not intend them to enjoy popular, commercial success.

An overview of the writing inside and outside the Boom does indicate that by the end of the 1960s the aesthetics of modernism were pervasive in the Latin American novel. Indeed, on the international scene, not only were some of the most talented masters of this modern form the recognized figures of the Boom but also several others were using the Spanish and Portuguese languages in ways never before imagined, even by Cervantes or Machado de Assis.

# Part 3

# The Postmodern Novel

# 13

# *Introduction to Postmodern Fiction in Latin America*

The writing of the 1960s—both inside and outside the Boom—as well as the writing of Borges, had done much to set the stage for a more experimental postmodern fiction in Latin America. Guimarães Rosa's *The Devil to Pay in the Backlands*, Cortázar's *Hopscotch*, and Cabrera Infante's *Three Trapped Tigers* were important precedents to postmodern fiction in Latin America because these authors experimented with language itself in Joycean ways rarely seen before in the Spanish or Portuguese languages; this work with language as a subject in itself is particular to postmodern writing in Latin America.

In the 1970s, as readers and critics became aware of the demise of the Boom as a unified political and aesthetic project, there was a certain crisis in nomenclature: what should the literature written after the Boom be called? As new writers appeared on the scene in the 1970s and 1980s, several critics began speaking of a "post-Boom" of the Latin American novel. The next generation of talented writers, such as the Argentines Mempo Giardinelli and Luisa Valenzuela, were associated with this so-called post-Boom. As the heterogeneity of this writing became progressively more evident, however, the term post-Boom was increasingly seen as simplistic, reductive, and fundamentally unclear for any serious approach to the rich variety of literary phenomena apparent in Latin American fiction produced since the early 1970s.

At the same time, it became increasingly evident that an equally heterogeneous literary phenomenon in the West corresponded in many ways to what was being called postmodern fiction. By the early 1980s, it became more appropriate to describe the new novel in Latin America published since the late 1960s and early 1970s with a term that captured exactly what it was—postmodern fiction. Consequently, after some of the initial hesitation that accompanies the acceptance of most cultural change, there has been a growing recognition in U.S. academia and in Latin America of the idea of a postmodern novel in Latin America. The characteristics, definitions, and chronologies of this phenomenon are in the process of discussion and debate.[1] Much of the fiction published after the Boom by the two generations of writers, in fact, has characteristics that associate it with postmodern fiction in the West in general. This phenomenon has been particularly evident in Latin America since 1968, with the novels of Manuel Puig, Severo Sarduy, and others.

For Gabriel García Márquez and Latin American writing in general, *One Hundred Years of Solitude* represented a culmination, in 1967, of a modernist project. This literary production coincided with the growing complicity in First World academia between the formation and reproduction of the discipline of English (the dominant form of literary studies) and the very notion of modernism itself. García Márquez's modernist project was relatively late in arriving on the First World modernist scene. It was written almost exactly, in fact, at the time when John Barth began his postmodernist reflections on the literature of exhaustion, and when Leslie Fiedler, for better or for worse, popularized the term *postmodern*. With respect to a definition of the term, common concepts have been discontinuity, disruption, dislocation, decentering, indeterminacy, and antitotalization. As Linda Hutcheon points out, the cultural phenomenon of postmodernism is contradictory, for it installs and then subverts the very concepts it challenges.[2] Postmodernism works to subvert dominant discourses. In *The Dismemberment of Orpheus,* Ihab Hassan was instrumental in developing a critical language and concepts for postmodernism, creating parallel columns that place characteristics of modernism and postmodernism side by side. As Hutcheon points out, however, this "either/or" thinking suggests a resolution of what should be seen as unresolvable contradictions within postmodernism.

Differing concepts of postmodernism are articulated most prominently by Jean-Francois Lyotard, Jean Baudrillard, and Fredric Jameson. These three theorists are interested primarily in the analysis of culture and society in the postindustrial North Atlantic nations, and all three frequently equate postindustrial with postmodern. Lyotard's oft-cited *The Postmodern Condition: A Report on Knowledge* (1979) is an essay on the state of knowledge in postindustrial society. Lyotard maintains that we are now living at the end of the "grand narrative" or master narrative, such as the master narratives of science, the nation-state, the proletariat, the party, and the like, all of which have lost their viability. In postmodern culture, according to Lyotard, "The grand narrative has lost its credibility, regardless of what mode of unification it uses, regardless of whether it is a speculative narrative or a narrative of emancipation."[3]

Postmodern society, as viewed by Baudrillard, shares many of the proposals of Lyotard. In *Simulations*, Baudrillard proposes that the real is no longer real, but the order of the hyperreal and of simulation. Questioning the existence of any difference between the true and the false, Baudrillard rejects the discourses of truth of the hermeneutic tradition by making statements such as "We are in a logic of simulation which has nothing to do with a logic of facts and an order of reasons."[4] According to Baudrillard, "this anticipation . . . is what each time allows for all the possible interpretations, even the most contradictory—all are true, in the sense that their truth is exchangeable, in the image of the models from which they proceed, in a generalised cycle."[5] Baudrillard's postmodern world is one in which everything is seemingly exchangeable and nothing holds intrinsic value. In contemporary Latin American fiction, Baudrillard is not the subject of parody, but of pastiche, in the hands of writers such as Diamela Eltit.

Jameson describes postindustrial society in terms of a loss of history, the dissolution of the centered self, and the fading of individual style. He views postmodernism as a result of the capitalist dissolution of bourgeois hegemony and the development of mass culture. In general, Jameson is skeptical of the postmodern enterprise and is often critical of postmodern fiction. For example, one of the characteristics he attributes to postmodernism is pastiche, or the random cannibalization of all the styles of the past, the play of random stylistic allusion. For Jameson, pastiche is a negative, while Hutcheon and others view such phenomena as examples of the inherent contradictions that are essential to postmodernism. In Latin American fiction, the pastiche need not be seen in a negative light.

For a reading of Latin American postmodern fiction, the politics of postmodernism are an extremely important issue. Hutcheon argues against the critical postures Jameson takes toward a postmodernism that he sees as politically suspicious because of its lack of historicism. She argues in favor of a postmodern novel that is indeed historical and gives numerous examples of postmodern novels with strong historical components. Her answer to Jameson is that the past as referent is not bracketed or effaced, but given new and different life and meaning. For Hutcheon, then, the postmodern novel does not strive for the truth, as Jameson might wish, but deals with truths and questions the conditions under which truths are established.

As poststructuralist thinkers who have had enormous impact on postmodern literary culture in general, Michel Foucault and Jacques Derrida have also been quite influential in Latin America. Foucault attempted to establish the location of power in literary texts and rethought the subject as a discursive construct. Derrida questioned the concept of center as well as the possibilities of history capturing a way to truth. Obviously playing off Foucault and Derrida on the matter of a text's subject, the *Tel Quel* group in Paris organized an attack on the founding subject or concept of author. The Cuban Severo Sarduy, a member of the *Tel Quel* group, questions the idea of subject and then proceeds to parody Derrida in his novel *Cobra* (1972). Sarduy is frequently cited by the Latin American postmodern writers, including Diamela Eltit and R. H. Moreno-Durán.

Writing about contemporary fiction in general, Hutcheon is interested in the contradictions of postmodernism. Citing Larry McCaffery, she begins her definition of postmodernism by referring to literature that is metafictionally self-reflective and yet speaks to us powerfully about real political and historical realities. For Hutcheon, the key concepts for postmodernism are paradox, contradiction, and a movement toward antitotalization, all of which appear throughout her books *A Poetics of Postmodernism* and *The Politics of Postmodernism*. The concepts of the multiple, the provisional, and the different are also important for Hutcheon.

Hutcheon proposes that the term *postmodernism* in fiction be reserved for what she calls "historiographic metafiction." This postmodern fiction, as she describes it, often enacts the problematic nature of writing history to narrativization, raising questions about the cognitive status of historical knowledge. It "refuses the view that only history has a truth claim, both by questioning the ground of that claim in historiography and by discourses, human constructs, signifying systems, and both derive their major claims to truth from that identity."[6] Historiographic metafiction suggests that *truth* and *falsity* may not be the right terms. Rather, we should be speaking of truths in the plural.

Umberto Eco claims that the postmodern is born at the moment when we discover that the world has no fixed center and that, as

Foucault taught, power is not something unitary that exists outside of us. This moment occurred in Latin American literature with the rise of Borges, who became a seminal figure for many European theorists and Latin American postmodern novelists in the 1960s and 1970s, even though the now-classic Borges fiction they were reading dated back to the 1940s. The two books that contained these groundbreaking stories were *The Garden of Forking Paths* (1941) and *Ficciones* (1944). One of the repeated images in Borges's fiction was the labyrinth as a centerless universe, a figure developed in stories such as "The Library of Babel" and "The Garden of Forking Paths"; this image is elaborated most directly in "The Library of Babel." In "The Circular Ruins," language has priority over empirical reality, as the protagonist, who has the power to dream a person into being, realizes at the end that he, too, is an illusion—that someone else was dreaming him. Consequently, the imagined reality of dreams, which are figments of the imagination, and language, which is the written product of the imagination, are both more powerful than empirical reality.

Borges's "The Library of Babel" and "Pierre Ménard, Author of the *Quixote*" are also foundational texts for postmodern fiction in Latin America. In them, the line between essay and fiction is blurred, opening the gates for the fictionalized theoretical prose of Ricardo Piglia, Severo Sarduy, José Balza, José Emilio Pacheco, and several others.

Some critics view Borges's writing as too autonomous and independent from sociopolitical reality and conservative as a literary project. Borges's fiction often functions on the basis of an abstract rather than Argentine or Latin American referent. Nevertheless, Borges's literary discourse operates in a way similar to what Hutcheon notes in other postmodern writers: the narrator's discourse is paradoxically postmodern, for it both inscribes a context and then contests its boundaries.

A concept of what exactly constitutes the postmodern in Latin America is just as polemical among critics of Latin American culture. Despite the initial doubts of Joaquín Brunner, Adolfo Sánchez Vásquez, and a few others, Latin American society and culture have experienced the same crisis of truth that Lyotard, Baudrillard, and Jameson describe as existing in the North Atlantic nations. With the breakdown of the grand narratives of the nation-state, Latin America's traditional ruling classes now respond to the same multinational companies, corporate leaders, high-level administrators, and the like that Lyotard describes as the new rulers of the North Atlantic nations.

The discourse and concepts of First World postmodernism are now circulating in Latin America—*lo indeterminado* (the indeterminate), *la problematización del centro* (the problematization of the center), *la marginalidad* (marginality), *la descontinuidad* (discontinuity), *la simulación* (simulation), and the like. One of Diamela Eltit's common terms, *precariedad* (precarious) is similar to *the provisional*, which is emphasized by many of the North Atlantic postmodern intellectuals. Perhaps the word North and South postmoderns share the most, however—with no translation necessary—is *Borges*. The same Borges who was cited by the European poststructuralist theorists Barthes, Foucault, Baudrillard, and Lyotard also planted the seeds for a Latin American postmodern fiction with his stories of the 1940s.

After Borges, the most notable contributions to the later publication of a Latin American postmodern fiction were Guimarães Rosa's *The Devil to Pay in the Backlands* and Cortázar's *Hopscotch*. Cortázar's novel in itself was not fully a postmodern work, but its Morelli chapters at the end of the book were a radical proposal for postmodern fiction (see chapter 9 in the present volume). In the late 1960s and early 1970s, the postmodern novel began to appear in Latin America, almost always inspired by either Borges or Cortázar, and it was constituted by such experimental fictions as Cabrera Infante's *Three Trapped Tigers* (1967), Néstor Sánchez's *Siberia Blues* (1967), and Manuel Puig's *Betrayed by Rita Hayworth* (1968). As mentioned, another key novel for the formation of a Latin American postmodern was Severo Sarduy's *Cobra* (1972).

Soon several other radically experimental novelists appeared on the Latin American scene—most of them after Sarduy—including the Argentines Ricardo Piglia, Reina Roffé, and Héctor Libertella; the Mexicans Salvador Elizondo, Carmen Boullosa, and José Emilio Pacheco; the Colombians R. H. Moreno-Durán and Albalucía Angel; the Venezuelan José Balza; and Diamela Eltit of Chile. Eltit followed the linguistic innovations offered by Sarduy, except for parody, which she openly rejects. These writers offer radically different kinds of postmodernisms—perhaps a postmodern phenomenon in itself: if *Culture* (with a capital *C* and singular) becomes cultures in postmodernity, as Hutcheon has suggested, then the provisionality and heterogeneity of postmodern cultures in Latin America will be even more extreme than in the North Atlantic nations. For the most part, these Latin American postmodern writers, like their First World counterparts, are interested in heterogeneous discourses of theory and literature. Sarduy's essays read like fiction and vice versa; Eltit's fiction appropriates the theoretical discourse of Derrida, Baudrillard, Deleuze, and others. Balza prefers not to distinguish between the essays and the fiction of his "exercises."

Many Latin American women share with their First World counterparts what Hutcheon calls the postmodern valuing of the margins. The postmodern women novelists in Latin America frequently write with a self-conscious awareness of feminist and poststructuralist theory. This is the case with Albalucía Angel, whose recent novels incorporate the language of feminist theory, as do the writings of the Brazilian Helena Parente Cunha, as well as those of Sylvia Molloy, Diamela Eltit, and others. Indeed, the rise of feminist writing in Latin America in the 1980s is one of the most notable literary phenomena since the Boom.

Numerous scholars have observed the postmoderns' bridging of the gap between elite and popular art. Since the 1960s, the Latin American writers who have been the object of intense academic study have, at the same time, frequently been best-sellers, particularly García Márquez, Vargas Llosa, Isabel Allende, Luis Rafael Sánchez, and Manuel Puig. Three works that have sold particularly well to both the general public and to academe (and seemingly bridged the gap between elite and popular art) are Vargas Llosa's *Aunt Julia and the Script Writer* (1977), Allende's *House of the Spirits* (1982), and García Márquez's *Chronicle of a Death Foretold* (1981)— novels that could arguably be called, for different reasons, postmodern. For Hutcheon, postmodernism's relationship with contemporary mass culture is not just one of implication but also one of critique. This critical position toward mass culture is particularly evident in *Aunt Julia and the Script Writer* and Luis Rafael Sánchez's *Macho Camacho's Beat*. Jameson tends to categorize postmodern fiction in terms of mass culture, limiting the postmodern to what might be considered its "lighter" versions.

In a recent study of postmodernism and popular culture, Angela McCrobbie suggests that recent debates on postmodernism possess both a positive attraction and a usefulness to the analyst of popular culture.[7] Citing the work of Andreas Huyssen, McCrobbie notes the "high" structuralist preference for the works of high modernism, especially the writing of James Joyce or Stephan Mallarmé. Postmodernism, in contrast, has been more interested in popular culture than the canonical works of literary modernism. McCrobbie also draws parallels between Susan Sontag's perspective on a camp sensibility and what Jameson calls pastiche.

One major difference between North Atlantic postmodernism, as it is articulated in the First World, and Latin American postmodernism centers on the issue of critique. Some critics, such as Jameson, consider North Atlantic postmodernism politically neutral or uncritical. Latin American postmodernism is as resolutely historical and inescapably political as Hutcheon asserts North American postmodernism is. This argument is perhaps stronger in the Latin American case because the historical and political have been consistently present in the entire tradition of the Latin American novel.

To cite the example of Diamela Eltit, her postmodern novelistic project was born in the 1980s, after she began participating in cultural and political activities that were part of an underground resistance in Pinochet's Chile during the 1970s and early 1980s. Her first two novels can be easily associated with the postmodernism of First World writers and Latin Americans such as Sarduy and Piglia. The first of these, *Lumpérica* (1983, Lumperica), takes place in a public plaza in Santiago, has no real plot, and has as protagonist a character named L. Iluminada. This plaza is the postmodern world of Baudrillard, where human beings have the same exchange value as merchandise.

Eltit's second novel, *Por la patria* (1986, For the patria), is even more markedly experimental. She alludes to the political repression of the Pinochet regime, always returning to the historical origins of language, repression, and resistance. In returning to medieval epic wars, she inevitably associates these historical conflicts with the contemporary situation. Consequently, Eltit's postmodern stance is patently historical and political and could be identified as an allegorical fiction of resistance. Her third novel, *The Fourth World* (1988), deals with family relationships and is related by two narrators: the first half of the work is narrated by a young boy, María Chipia, the son of the family, and the second half is told by his twin sister. *The Fourth World* is not a work that suggests the broad historical truths elaborated in novels of the Boom, such as *One Hundred Years of Soli-*

*tude* or *The Death of Artemio Cruz.* The generation of García Márquez and Fuentes remained not only overtly historical but also engaged in a project of the truths of social emancipation. *The Fourth World,* however, is about other kinds of truths—the truths of private and public space, the truths of relationships, the truths of the body, and a questioning of the possibilities language holds for articulating truths.

*The Fourth World* and other select Latin American postmodern novels question the truth industry of modernism. In Latin American fiction, the novel has moved from utopia to what Foucault calls heterotopia—from the centered and historical universe of the utopian Alejo Carpentier and García Márquez to a centerless universe of the postmoderns Sarduy and Eltit. What is at stake for the Latin American postmoderns who have arisen since the late 1960s—Pacheco, Sarduy, Moreno-Durán, Eltit, and others—is not truth. Lyotard claims that the question is no longer, "Is it true?" but "What use is it?" and "How much is it worth?"; the latter are questions posed in *The Fourth World* and in much of what might be called postmodern cultural practice in Latin America.

Latin American writers such as Eltit and Piglia share with North Atlantic postmoderns a generalized mistrust of the capacity of any language to render truths about the world. The discourse of truth has been reduced to exchange values. Consequently, the very exercise of considering the implications of hermeneutical philosophical discourse of truth claims becomes a suspicious activity in those cultural spaces of Latin America—spaces occupied by Sarduy, Piglia, Pacheco, Eltit, Valenzuela, and numerous others—where postmodernism organizes new discourses.

These new discourses—these new postmodernities—grow directly from modernist writing in Latin America: the writing of Borges, Asturias, Carpentier, Guimarães Rosa, García Márquez, and others. These discourses are cultural practices that represent a fundamental break from the past as recent as the 1940s, the 1950s, and the early 1960s. In another break from the Boom, the most innovative writers are, to a large extent, feminist writers.

# 14

# *Postmodern Fiction in South America*

## Introduction

Buenos Aires, Santiago, Rio de Janeiro, Bogotá, and Caracas are the centers of postmodern culture in South America, and the novelistic production of recent years reflects this geography.

South America has become one of the most intensely productive regions of postmodern fiction in Latin America. Postmodern writers such as Diamela Eltit, Sylvia Molloy, Ricardo Piglia, Alejandra Pizarnik, Héctor Libertella, and Armonía Sommers make the periphery of the Southern Cone region, paradoxically, a vital center of postmodern fictional creation. The most vibrant area of postmodern culture in the Andean region is Colombia, with writers such as Albalucía Angel and R. H. Moreno-Durán, while postmodern trends in Venezuela are centered in Caracas. Ecuador, Peru, and Bolivia have been bound historically to indigenous cultures, and so their modernization has come more slowly and with less progress than in Colombia and Venezuela. The postmodern sectors of their respective societies have been negligible.

## Argentina

Some critics might contend—with considerable justification—that Latin American postmodern fiction was born in Argentina with the publication of Borges's *Ficciones* in 1941. It embodies the self-conscious metafiction, indeterminacy, and unresolved contradiction, as well as other elements, that became so important for Latin American postmodern writers decades later. The first wave of writers after the Boom to create radically experimental and self-conscious works in Argentina included the young Néstor Sánchez, whose novel *Siberia Blues* (1967) has intrigued many critics since its publication. With *Siberia Blues*, Cortázar's *62: A Model Kit* (1968), Héctor Libertella's *El camino de los hiperbóreos* (1968, The road of southern nations), and the fiction of Manuel Puig, in addition to Humberto Costantini's *Háblenme de Funes* (1970, Speak to me of Funes), it was evident that Argentine fiction was undergoing a revolution, clearly a break from the modernist tradition that had dominated since the 1940s. One of the most technically experimental works published in postmodern Argentina, *Siberia Blues* focuses on language itself for its structure and theme and on the construction of a sentence, which could well be the work's major event.

Several Argentine writers accepted Morelli's invitation in *Hopscotch* to create a novel more by the principles of chance than by reasoned logic. In chapter 62 of *Hopscotch*, Morelli suggests the possibility of creating a novel on the basis of random notes and observations. Cortázar himself pursues this idea in *62: A Model Kit* (see chapter 9 in this volume). This novel has entities who are only nominally "characters." Libertella does create a protagonist in *El camino de los hiperbóreos*, but there is no traditional sense of plot other than the protagonist's search for something undefined. In addition, Libertella subverts any concept of individual identity by creating a multiple identity in this character. In *Háblenme de Funes*, Costantini creates a structure consisting of three vaguely related stories, the third of which is a metafiction dealing with a writer's creative process.

The postmodern fiction of Manuel Puig, which he initiated with the experimental *Betrayed by Rita Hayworth* (1968), consists of eight novels. This novel established a postmodern reader who necessarily had an active and unstable role to play, for there is no controlling narrator to organize the anecdotal material that is related by a multiplicity of voices appearing in the text as monologues or dialogues. This narrative, about how imported popular culture can construct identity, is a typically postmodern text: there is neither a privileged narrator upon whom the reader can rely for complete information nor an authoritative discourse or figure to whom we can turn for something like an objective, final truth regarding its fiction.[1]

All of Puig's novels contain narrative structures, fictionalized postmodern readers, and themes similar to those in *Betrayed by Rita Hayworth*. His later work critiques gender-bound behavior and genre-bound thinking, particularly *Heartbreak Tango* (1969), *The*

*Buenos Aires Affair* (1973), and *The Kiss of the Spider Woman* (1976). They all deal also with questions of authority and power.

A second wave of postmodern fiction in Argentina has been produced by writers well aware of their debts to Borges, Cortázar, and postmodern culture in general. Among the most prominent of this second wave are Ricardo Piglia, Héctor Libertella, Sylvia Molloy, and Alejandra Pizarnik.

Piglia has written four books of fiction that, in their totality, represent one of the most aesthetically innovative and politically significant projects since the writings of Cortázar. More appropriately read as one body of fiction than as four separate books, Piglia's works are *Assumed Name* (1975), *Artificial Respiration* (1979), *Prisión perpetua* (1988, Perpetual prison), and *La ciudad ausente* (1992, The absent city). They are fictions that can be best read as fictional meditations. As political essays, they represent a rewriting of Argentine history—both political history and literary history.

Piglia's first volume of stories, *Assumed Name,* can also be read as a novel. It begins with a quotation from the Argentine novelist Roberto Arlt ("The only things that we lose are those that we never really had."), an authorial note by Piglia, and six stories. The book is populated by marginalized and often frail and aging characters. They live anguished lives in their attempts to understand their circumstance by deciphering the written and spoken word. In "The End of the Ride," Emilio Renzi takes a bus trip to visit his dying father in a hospital. During the trip, he befriends a solitary woman who claims to be a former opera singer, Aída. After his father dies in the hospital, Renzi goes to Aída's apartment. "Mousy Benítez Sang Boleros" details the relationship between two over-the-hill and hopeless boxers. "The Madwoman and the Story of a Crime" is a superb story that deals with not only a man's loss of a woman but also the creation of fiction. The title story, "Assumed Name," is a lengthy and complex text with two parts. The first, "Homage to Roberto Arlt," is Piglia's "report" or "abstract" concerning the supposed ownership of a text by Arlt. Part 2, "Appendix: Luba," is a story supposedly printed from an unpublished manuscript that Piglia found. The issues of ownership and authorship, however, are just as ambiguous at the end as they were in the beginning. This volume reads like a series of essays and, to a certain extent, must be read as (metaphorical) political essays about authority and power, as well as implicit critiques of the uses of political power in Argentina.

*Artificial Respiration* begins with the question, "Is there a story?" Piglia then keeps the reader engaged with this matter for the remainder of the novel, even though the action is minimal. In the original Spanish, this question "¿Hay una historia?" carries the double meaning of, "Is there a story?" and "Is there history?" thus suggesting one of the major issues of the novel—the relationship between literature and history. Read in this manner, *Artificial Respiration* is a 200-page meditation on Argentine cultural and political history. It consists of two parts, the first of which is narrated by a Pole named Vladimir Tardewski living in Argentina. Part 1 deals with Enrique Ossorio, a private secretary of the nineteenth-century dictator Juan Manuel Rosas. Emilio Renzi, who appeared in *Assumed Name*, collaborates with his uncle, Marcelo Maggi, to reconstruct the life of Ossorio. In part 2 the focus changes to a lengthy conversation (from 10:00 A.M. until the following dawn) between Maggi's friend Tardewski and Renzi. Their dialogue on literature includes a supposed encounter between Hitler and Kafka in Prague around 1909.

In this novel, Piglia considers the question of how national histories are constructed and institutionalized. It returns to the roots of Argentine nationhood in the nineteenth century and fuses national history and family history. Tardewski himself is a cultural statement, for he is the Argentine intellectual par excellence: a European who is situated on the periphery (in the province of Entre Ríos) speculating about European culture as it interacts with Argentine literature.

This novel also sets forth the issue of *patria* and language. Lengthy discussions on Argentine literature bring to bear Piglia's position on the notions of *patria* and language. On the one hand, the characters are highly critical of the turn-of-the-century poet Leopoldo Lugones, a literary icon who has been institutionalized in Argentina. Lugones is criticized as a national poet with the most "pure language," who thus can be associated implicitly with the "sanitization" process of the military dictatorships of the 1970s. Arlt, on the other hand, is much admired by the characters in *Artificial Respiration* and represents the opposite of Lugones, for Arlt's language can be characterized as often crude, clumsy, even vulgar. By criticizing Lugones and praising Arlt, Piglia critiques the very foundations of the traditional Argentine concept of *patria*.

Piglia's other two books of fiction, *Prisión perpetua* and *La ciudad ausente*, develop many of the same issues introduced in *Artificial Respi-*

*ration. Prisión perpetua* is less a novel than a set of 10 fictions—that are related but that escape the classification of short stories for most readers—some of which had appeared previously in *Assumed Name*. Piglia pushes the concept of the active (post-*Hopscotch*) reader to its extreme in *Prisión perpetua*. Part 3 of this book consists of a double-coded meta-plagiarism.[2] In his "Homenaje a Roberto Arlt" in part 3, Piglia claims that he is publishing an unpublished text of Arlt's. In reality, the text that follows "Luba" is a slightly altered version of a Russian short story entitled "The Dark" by Leonid Andreyen (obviously not reproduced in the mother tongue in *Prisión perpetua*). Ellen McCracken shows how the active postmodern reader is urged to become a detective to find the textual clues to Piglia's metaplagiarism. She concludes that by performing the detective work, readers can arrive at the truth behind the literary puzzle of the story.[3] The postmodern reader is invited to be "aggressive" (to use McCracken's term).

In *La ciudad ausente* (1992), Piglia reaffirms his invitation to the postmodern reader to decipher the unspeakable, which is written in a language always at least once removed from the mother tongue. The novel is Piglia's rewriting of the Argentine writer Macedonio Fernández (whom he names constantly in the text) and his story of a machine located in a museum that narrates stories. Two elements in *La ciudad ausente* associate Piglia's fiction to other postmodern writers in Latin America. On the one hand, the machine "narrates in a foreign language," thus underlining the tendency of Piglia to narrate in a language other than the mother tongue, Spanish. On the other, *La ciudad ausente* is what one critic has called a paranoiac tale.[4] Characters in such stories interpret the world as a complex series of intrigues, plots, and arbitrary signs that always hide a play with power. If knowledge is used to guarantee access to truth, the excess of information distances us from truth and places us in the paranoia of deciphering signs. In *La ciudad ausente*, several characters are obsessed with deciphering signs and putting order to the stories.

Like Piglia, Héctor Libertella writes postmodern works that often blur traditional boundaries between fiction and essay. Two of his recent books are more like essays than fictional exercises. In his theory of fiction (and fiction of theory) presented in *Las sagradas escrituras* (1993, The sacred writings), Libertella posits what he identifies as a "lyrical criticism." In this writing, the two figures to whom he returns continually are the postmodern writers Enrique Lihn from Chile and Salvador Elizondo from Mexico. Writing as a postmodern observer of society, Libertella suggests that the Americas are nothing more than a geographical, political, and literary network in accordance with how and why other disciplines want to appropriate them. The heterodox and provocative essays in *Las sagradas escrituras* lead Libertella and the reader to question the ontological status of the Spanish language and nationhood in Argentina.

Libertella continues his ongoing questioning of the viability of the Spanish language and writing in *El paseo internacional del perverso* (1990, The international trip of the perverse one). It is a short novel that attempts to subvert its status as a novel and an example of any fixed language; and it also attempts to avoid any fixed subject, for the main character, an itinerant entity who travels around the world, never takes on any fixed identity.

Sylvia Molloy and Alejandra Pizarnik are authors of subtle fictions that are testimony to the heterogeneity of postmodern writing in Argentina and the different ways postmodern writers of this region can be political. Molloy's *Certificate of Absence* (1981) returns to the postmodern origins of Borges, the Borges who offers reflections on the text, questioning the stability of the text itself. It is a self-conscious and feminist text that defends its marginality and refuses to comply with many of the expectations traditional readers may have of masculine texts. It deals with an Argentine woman who returns to an apartment in New England where she had once had an affair with another woman and where she writes a memoir about the experience. She struggles with her means of expression; her self-conscious rereading of her writing makes this novel comparable to much postmodern fiction. Some critics have contended that a good portion of feminist fiction is necessarily constructed on the basis of fragments. Molloy claims that she always planned to write in fragments because she never thought in terms of total blocks of material. *Certificate of Absence*, in fact, is a group of fragments that she started writing and organizing into a novel in the early 1970s.[5] She also recognizes that the novel is written in the same voice as some of her work on Borges, a fact that aligns her closely to the writing of Piglia and other postmodern writers in Latin America.[6]

Alejandra Pizarnik is known in Argentina and Latin America as an accomplished poet. In her one short novel (or long short story) entitled *The Bloody Countess* (1971), Pizarnik revisits a Dracula story, but it is set in a postmodern world in which neither the moral nor the immoral are factors; morality is simply not an issue.

Postmodern writing in Argentina—which includes Piglia, Libertella, Molloy, Pizarnik, and several others—works to subvert dominant historical and literary discourses. In this sense, these writers are among the most profoundly political in Latin America. Paraphrasing Kafka and Arlt, Piglia's fiction poses the question of how to speak the unspeakable in a repressive military regime. Molloy and Pizarnik, on the other hand, offer new feminist voices in opposition to the dominant discourses of patriarchy.

# Brazil

The interests of Brazilian writers in the modern and postmodern have roots in the 1920s. Brazil initiated an effort to modernize its culture by organizing Semana de Arte Moderna (Modern Art Week) in São Paulo in 1922, a turning point in Brazilian cultural history. The event brought the European avant-garde movements of the time to the consciousness of Brazil's intellectuals and literati. One result of this cultural change was the fiction of Oswald de Andrade, who was influenced by the cubists and futurists, an influence that was displayed in his canonical novels *Memórias sentimentais de João Miramar* (1924, Sentimental memories of João Miramar) and *Seraphim Ponte Grande* (1933). Contemporary fiction has taken a plethora of directions in Brazil, from highly experimental postmodern works to science fiction, pulp novels, murder mysteries, and adventure narratives.

The leading postmodern fiction writers in Brazil have been Clarice Lispector, Ignácio de Loyola Brandão, Roberto Drummond, Rubem Fonseca, Ivan Ângelo, and Flávio Moreira de Costa. A writer from the earlier generation, Osman Lins, published a landmark novel for postmodern fiction in Brazil, *Avalovara* (1973). It is a work in the form of a series of narrative fragments and it contains many of the elements proposed by Morelli in *Hopscotch*. Lispector, like Fuentes and Vargas Llosa, was fundamentally a modernist writer who was affected by the postmodern later in her career. Her feminist work *The Hour of the Star* is a metafiction that deals with the creative process and fictionalizes an active postmodern reader.[7]

One of the most experimental of the Brazilian postmodern writers is Loyola Brandão, author of *Zero* (1974), one of the most innovative works to be published in Brazil in the early 1970s. It invites comparisons with postmodern Latin American fictions such as Cortázar's *A Manual for Manuel* and Piglia's *Artificial Respiration*, because the relationship between a police interrogator and his captive is portrayed as a complex game to be deciphered only by the most engaged postmodern reader. Loyola Brandão's *Não verá país nenhum* (1982, You will see no country) is a futuristic novel in which the author openly recognizes his literary masters, including Isaac Asimov, Ray Bradbury, and Kurt Vonnegut. With frequent black humor, Loyola Brandão communicates a sense of exhaustion on the part of Brazilian society, a feeling that pervades much postmodern fiction published in that country since the early 1970s.

Roberto Drummond appropriates the popular culture of the Mardi Gras in *Sangue de Coca-Cola* (1983, Coca-Cola Blood), in which he integrates popular music with a rewriting of the recent history of Brazil's military dictatorship. Rubem Fonseca's *Bufo & Spallanzani* (1985) is a parody of detective fiction, with a character who is a compulsive writer in the process of creating a book—entitled *Bufo & Spallanzani*. *A festa* (1976, The celebration), by Ivan Angelo, is experimental in technique and leaves the postmodern reader the task of rewriting official history. It is conceived with a free-floating narrative focus, a Cortázarian openness.[8] Flávio Moreira da Costa's *O deastraonauta: OK Jack Kerouac nós estamos te esperando em Copacabana* (1971, The antiastronaut: O. K. Jack Kerouac, we are waiting for you in Copacabana) is a metafiction with the irreverent and rebellious attitude of the fiction of Gustavo Sainz and José Agustín in Mexico in the 1960s.

Brazil is a country with a vast and diverse novelistic production; consequently, numerous other writers with postmodern tendencies need to be mentioned. Márcio Souza is not generally as innovative as novelists such as Loyola Brandão, Molloy, or Piglia, but his novel *Mad Maria* (1982) is a political novel that one critic has described as an ontological journey.[9] Souza, like many modernists in Latin America (and unlike most postmodern writers), searches to understand human relationships and truths, both of which find more substantive possibilities than in most postmodern fiction.

# Chile

An early indicator of an imminent Chilean postmodern fiction appeared in 1968, the same year as similar signs emerged in Argentina and much of Latin America. This narrative innovation was an experimental and relatively obscure novel entitled *Job-Boj*, published in 1968 by Jorge Guzmán, who until then was better known as a scholar of Spanish literature than a writer. Nevertheless, Guzmán's invitation to experiment with the postmodern, accompanied by the international revolution in theory (which came earlier and stronger to the Southern Cone nations than to the United States), an international postmodern fiction, and the repressive military dictatorship of Pinochet (among other factors) led to the publication of the radical fictions of Mauricio Wacquez and Enrique Lihn. Guzmán's *Job-Boj*, the José Donoso of *The Obscene Bird of the Night* (1970), and the radical fictions of Wacquez and Lihn represent a first wave of Chilean postmodern fiction, followed by a second wave consisting of Diamela Eltit, Alberto Fuguet, Antonio Ostornol, Ariel Dorfman, and the Donoso of *The Garden Next Door* (1981) and *Taratuta/Still Water with Pipe* (1990).

Recognized internationally as a poet, Lihn also wrote radically experimental novels that went generally unnoticed outside of Chile, except by postmodern writers of equally hermetic tendencies, such as the Argentine Héctor Libertella. Writing on Lihn's two novelistic books, *La orquesta de cristal* (1976, The crystal orchestra) and *El arte de la palabra* (1980, The art of the word), Libertella proposes that Lihn's work with literary discourse is an attempt to critique the excessive rhetoric of the "dead" Spanish language by distancing his own discourse from it. Lihn finds he needs to write in hermetic codes to avoid the literal reproduction of the dominant discourses that become the object of parody and pastiche in his writing. Lihn thus identifies with the hermetic as a political strategy, according to Libertella. The multiple footnotes of *La orquesta de cristal* and the metadiscourse of *El arte de la palabra* make language the main subject of these two novels.

Eltit's postmodern project consists of the four novels *Lumpérica* (1983), *Por la patria* (1986, For the country), *The Fourth World* (1988), and *Sacred Cow* (1991). Julio Ortega has described these works as part of an ample reappropriation of the discourse of the figurative that various Latin American women writers have proposed.[10] Her first three books were written under Pinochet's dictatorship, and so Eltit joined other young novelists in the creation of a writing of resistance. Along with the work of Piglia and Fuentes's *Terra Nostra*, her total writing represents one of the most ambitious, challenging, and profound searches for historical origins recently published in Latin America. Each of the 10 chapters in *Lumpérica* takes a radically different narrative strategy, with different types of language, organization, and even typography. The experimentation becomes more intense as the novel develops, and chapters near the end become so experimental that their main subject is language itself. A minimal sense of coherence is created by the fact that the last chapter returns to the situation of the first, with the central character (L. Iluminada) alone in the plaza absorbed in contemplation.

*Lumpérica* is the first of Eltit's texts on the body. In this novel, she writes about and explores the body under conditions of extreme pain.[11] L. Iluminada is the sum of a body that finds itself at the limits of death. Reduced to a minimal concept of "character," L. Iluminada is a fragment of a name with minimal contextual information. Given no past and no motives, the postmodern reader is forced to construct a story written in the margins of the female body.

Eltit's *Por la patria* is one of the most radical experiments published in Latin America in recent decades. Julio Ortega says that in this novel "the communitarian is the feminine subjective space of the subversive."[12] Eltit relates a story of contemporary Chile, particularly the politically repressive Pinochet regime, but she always returns to the historical origins of language, repression, and resistance. In recalling medieval epic wars, she inevitably associates these historical conflicts with the contemporary situation. Consequently, Eltit's postmodern stance is markedly historical and political. By exploring the origins of the mother language (Spanish) and incorporating numerous historical and colloquial languages into *Por la patria*, Eltit is concerned with the relationship that was originally explored by Foucault between language and power and that is the subject of much of Piglia's writing.

Eltit also explores the concept of linguistic excess in *Por la patria*. This issue relates to the fact that postmodern fiction poses new questions about reference. As Linda Hutcheon points out, the issue is no longer, "To what empirically real object in the past does the language of history refer?"; it is more, "To which discursive context could this language belong?" and "To which prior textualization must we refer?"[13] *Lumpérica* and *Por la patria* reveal a sense for origins in the Latin language, the "mother" language of the later Romance language family, which is present in both novels. The discursive contexts change in the different fragments of *Lumpérica*, evoking a connection with the past heritage in Latin and resonances of medieval Spanish and Italian. These historical languages coexist, in an unresolved contradiction, with a modern masculine discourse subverted by other contemporary discourses—colloquial Chilean Spanish and feminine discourse. The juxtaposition of these languages could be seen as incest among the elements in the linguistic family inhabiting this novel as well as a questioning of the possibility of writing in the mother tongue.

The "fourth world" of Eltit's novel *The Fourth World* can be postulated as a space consisting of a periphery of a periphery, for example, marginal space on the periphery of an already peripheral Third World nation. Written under the Pinochet regime, Eltit's work offers an allegorical level of reading. The four novels that make up Eltit's postmodern project can be approached by the postmodern reader as allegories of resistance. *Sacred Cow*, like *Lumpérica*, and *The Fourth World*, is a transgressive text written in the margins and on the body in an unstable space that frequently evokes the unspeakable.

Eltit has spoken about the "scene of power" as well as the ideology of the body in interviews and in her books of fiction. Her response to these scenes of power is a transgressive and irreverent fiction of cultural resistance. As Guillermo García Corales has observed, Eltit offers no solutions to power relations in Chile or elsewhere.[14] Rather, she forces the often uncomfortable postmodern reader of her texts to question the cultural and political constructs that legitimate power. Her writing on the female body is one of her several mechanisms for questioning authoritative discourses.

After Eltit, the young practitioners of Chilean postmodern fiction are Antonio Ostornol (born in 1954) and Alberto Fuguet (born in 1964). In his third novel, *Los años de la serpiente* (1991, The years of the serpent), Ostornol challenges the postmodern reader with a variety of languages and texts that only vaguely constitute something like a novel. Fuguet's *Mala onda* (1991, Bad wave) is a fictionalized testimonial of postmodern Chile under Pinochet's regime, written in the hip language of Chile's alienated youth of the dictatorship.

# Colombia

As in Argentina and Chile, the postmodern turn in fiction in Colombia dates from the year 1968. Colombian postmodern fiction can be most clearly identified in the novel *Mateo el flautista* (1968, Mateo the flute player) by Alberto Duque López. The most accomplished postmodern innovators to appear on the scene in the 1970s were Albalucía Angel and R. H. Moreno-Durán, followed in the 1980s and 1990s by Darío Jaramillo Agudelo and Héctor Abad Faciolince.

Angel's postmodern feminist project consists of two works, *Misiá señora* (1982, Ms. Lady) and *Las andariegas* (1984, The travelers), novels that emanate directly from feminist theory and fiction. They are also her most hermetic works. *Misiá señora* deals with different aspects of female sexuality and gender issues. The fictional world of this novel creates a tenuous line between empirical reality and pure imagination. An important aspect of this richly imaginative experience is the creation of a new feminist discourse as part of Angel's feminist project. *Las andariegas* is a radical experiment that can be read as a double search: on the one hand, a search for a female language; on the other, an evocation of feminine identity. As in the fiction of Moreno-Durán and many postmoderns of Angel's generation, language is the principal subject in *Las andariegas*. Much of the narrative consists of brief phrases with unconventional punctuation often functioning as images. The use of verbal imagery in the novel is supported by visual images—a set of 12 drawings of a female body. Angel also experiments with the physical space of language, often in a manner similar to concrete poetry. Four pages of this typographical representation offer a variety of circular and semicircular arrangements with the names of famous women. The total effect of this visual imagery is to associate the body of the text with the female body. *Las andariegas* ends with a type of epilogue—a quotation from Monique Wittig—consisting of four brief sentences calling precisely for the project that is the radical essence of these two novels: a new language, a new beginning, a new history for women.

R. H. Moreno-Durán published a hermetic trilogy entitled *Fémina Suite* in the late 1970s and early 1980s, followed by two more novels. He writes essays as a citizen of international postmodern culture first and of Colombia second. His literary masters were Cervantes, the European moderns (particularly Robert Musil and Pierre Klossosky), Borges, Cortázar, and the Mexican Juan García Ponce. He also has considerable interest in the American innovators, from Ron Sukenick to William Gass and Robert Coover. The roots of *Fémina Suite* are found not in the empirical reality of Colombia but rather, as is the case with much postmodern fiction, in modernist literature.

Several factors unify this trilogy into a single postmodern project, but, above all, the role of language itself is the main subject of all three books.

Moreno-Durán's *Los felinos del Canciller* (1985, The felines of the chancellor) lacks some of the hermetic qualities of his previous work and much postmodern fiction. In this connection one might speak of an early postmodern attitude in the Andean region that produced relatively inaccessible works (the early Moreno-Durán, in this sense, corresponds to the early Severo Sarduy in Cuba and the early Néstor Sánchez in Argentina), in addition to a later, more accessible postmodern fiction. The difficulties and inaccessibility of many postmodern texts are replaced in *Los felinos del Canciller* by wit: rather than functioning as a barrier, Moreno-Durán's subtle manipulation of language is frequently the material of humor. This novel tells a family history, but only a superficial reading would emphasize it: the most important referents and the main subject of this postmodern novel are language and writing. The verb that captures the essence of the novel's action is "to manipulate." Indeed, the art of diplomacy, as practiced by the Barahona family, is the art of manipulation. More significant to the experience of this novel, however, is the manipulation of language, for if diplomacy is the protagonist's profession, philology is his passion.

The equivalencies between language and diplomacy in this novel lead to entertaining consequences. The text's postmodernism is signaled by the fact that, in the end, not just diplomacy but everything becomes the art of language and writing. That is, unique equivalencies are created between language and sexuality, between language and politics, and finally between language and writing.

Darío Jaramillo Agudelo has published two novels, *La muerte de Alec* (1983, The death of Alec) and *Cartas cruzadas* (1995, Crossed letters), both of which are epistolary narratives that fully engage the active postmodern reader. *La muerte de Alec* is a metafiction, a self-conscious meditation on the function of literature. As an epistolary novel, it is directed to an unidentified "you," one of the characters implicated with Alec. This you and the letter writer are friends of Alec, who dies during an excursion. The characters are Colombian, but the novel is set in the United States; and the letter writer is a novelist in the University of Iowa Writers' Program. Jaramillo Agudelo inverts the commonly accepted relationship between empirical reality and fiction: according to the narrator, it is not literature but life that is artificial, baroque, twisted. Similarly, the acts of storytelling (giving order to a story) and interpretation (giving meaning to a story) become the predominant forces, taking precedence over other forms of understanding reality. *Cartas cruzadas* involves a complex network of letters and diaries that give the reader a certain sense of Colombian society in the 1960s, but Jaramillo Agudelo's main interest is actually a self-reflective consideration of writing and literary theory.

Héctor Abad Faciolince's first novel, *The Joy of Being Awake* (1994), shares some of the attitudes of Moreno-Durán and Jaramillo Agudelo, while functioning on the same uncertain terrain of many other postmodern writers. Like Moreno-Durán, Abad Faciolince cultivates the art of digression. *The Joy of Being Awake* is a self-conscious and narcissistic story of a 72-year-old man who narrates the vicissitudes of his life from the time he was an adolescent, using the model of the Spanish picaresque novel. Like several postmodern writers such as Piglia, Jaramillo Agudelo, and the Mexican Luis Arturo Ramos, Abad Faciolince creates a character who searches for signs and believes in a world of chance that is not limited by modern systems of rational thought.

Colombian postmodern fiction follows two basic directions. The first consists of the hermetic fictions of Angel and Moreno-Durán, which connect with the type of international postmodern fiction originally defined and promoted by Ihab Hassan and which is represented in Mexico by writers such as Salvador Elizondo and José Emilio Pacheco. They require an active, postmodern reader. A more popular and accessible cultural reevaluation that implies a writing of resistance is effected by a younger generation that includes Andrés Caicedo, Umberto Valverde, and Orietta Lozano. This second tendency can be associated with fiction as diverse as the early fiction of the Cuban Cabrera Infante and the postmodern project of resistance published by Eltit.

## Ecuador, Bolivia, Peru

Ecuador, Bolivia, and Peru are centers of neither postmodern culture in general nor postmodern fiction. A few postmodern writers are of Ecuadorian, Bolivian, and Peruvian nationality, with most of them living and writing abroad. The most prominent postmodern novels produced in this region, in fact, have been written by a modernist who occasionally engages in some literary exercises with a postmodern flavor—Mario Vargas Llosa.[15]

The central figures of postmodern fiction in Ecuador have been Jorge Enrique Adoum, Iván Eguez, and Abdón Ubidia. One of the most radically experimental novels of the Andean region and certainly one of the most innovative fictions ever published in Ecuador is Adoum's *Entre Marx y una mujer desnuda* (1976, Between Marx and a nude woman). A series of thoughts on the novel and the nation of Ecuador, it is an encyclopedic work comparable in some ways to Fuentes's most lengthy piece of postmodern writing, *Terra Nostra*. Both are anthologies of postmodern gestures, motifs, and narrative strategies. The similarities with *Terra Nostra* are not coincidences; Adoum shares with Fuentes direct roots with Joyce, Borges' *Ficciones,* and Cortázar's *Hopscotch.* Adoum's novel begins, in fact, with references to Joyce and *Hopscotch* on the very first page. The subject of the novel's opening passages is a self-reflexive metacommentary on how novels begin. The narrator questions the possibility of storytelling and explains from the first paragraph that the traditional methods of ordering a story will not be used. Later, he offers comments related to the aesthetics of modern and postmodern literature. But perhaps the most telling feature of *Entre Marx y una mujer desnuda* is not the beginning but the fact that the prologue begins on page 233 of a 311-page novel.

Despite the presence of Adoum, Ecuadorian fiction is generally traditionalist and minimally affected by the postmodern. Iván Eguez, who has published several volumes of fiction since the 1970s, has written two novels with postmodern tendencies. Abdón Ubidia has also published some fiction with postmodern traits. Postmodern fiction represents a small sector of Ecuador's cultural production. Nevertheless, the historiographic metafiction of Adoum makes him one of the strongest postmodern voices in the Andean region.

Neither Bolivia nor Peru are centers of postmodern fiction in Latin America. Renato Prada Oropeza, a Bolivian professor who teaches literature and literary theory in Mexico, has published some postmodern fiction. In Peru, Vargas Llosa has participated in some postmodern practices since the 1970s. For example, *Who Killed Palomino Molero?* can be read as a postmodern text in the sense that it is a parodic play within the genre of the spy thriller. Keith Booker has argued that much of Vargas Llosa's fiction can be read as postmodern.

# Uruguay

The postmodern writers of Uruguay who have followed paths suggested by Borges and Cortázar include Híber Conteris, Armonía Sommers, and Cristina Peri Rossi. As was the case throughout Latin America, this innovative and experimental fiction began to appear in Uruguay in the late 1960s. Conteris has written five novels and has not been as engaged in experimentation as much as Piglia or Libertella, but he has written under the sign of Cortázar. He wrote *Ten Percent of Life* in Spanish while a political prisoner from 1976 to 1983 during the military dictatorship. Like the fiction of Eltit, *Ten Percent of Life* is a postmodern allegory of resistance. As Santiago Colas has pointed out, this novel needs to be read with an awareness of the context of the discourses in which it was written: the predominant discourse of the military dictatorship and the discourse of detective fiction.[16] In the classic detective novel, the detective's conclusions should become irrevocable truths and avoid the fact that truths are mere constructs. Conteris, however, subverts the very idea of definitive truths in his metafiction, thus subverting classic detective fiction. The active postmodern reader finds political clues hidden in this detective novel, which becomes an allegorical fiction of resistance. The reader never really knows what happens, making this yet another novel of the Southern Cone region addressing the unspeakable.

The fiction of Sommers and Peri Rossi demonstrates both modernist and postmodern tendencies. Sommers's modernist fiction dates back to the 1950s, but her more postmodern writing includes short fiction and novels written in the 1980s, such as the novel *Sólo los elefantes encuentran mandrágora* (1983, Only elephants find mandragora). The feminist writing of Peri Rossi has consisted mostly of short fiction but she has also published the novels *El libro de mis primos* (1969, The book of my cousins) and *Ship of Fools* (1984). Peri Rossi's postmodern fiction blurs generic boundaries, is often discontinuous, and is an art of proliferation and digression. *Ship of Fools* is a metafiction that questions the boundaries between painting and fiction.

# Venezuela

The major figure for postmodern fiction in Venezuela is José Balza. He has published numerous volumes of fiction in various forms, including several books of different variations and combinations that he, like Moreno-Durán, considers his "exercises." His novels are *Marzo anterior* (1965, Previous March), *Largo* (1968, Long), *Setecientas palmeras plantadas en el mismo lugar* (1974, Seven-hundred palm trees planted in the same place), *D* (1987), *Percusión* (1982, Percussion), and *Medianoche en video: 1/5* (1988, Midnight on video: 1/5). Like Moreno-Durán and Piglia, Balza often blurs the line between fictional and essayistic discourses, writing fictions about literature and essays in a fictional mode. He outlines a theory of the novel in a lengthy essay on *Don Quixote* entitled *Este mar narrativo* (1987, This narrative sea) in which he refers to the usual literary father figures of the Latin American postmoderns: Joyce, Cervantes, Borges, and Cortázar. In this essay, he privileges the unresolved contradictions of the novel that are typical of postmodern fiction, and he often returns to the correlations between the body and writing. Balza's postmodern fiction consists of *D*, *Percusión*, and *Medianoche en video: 1/5*. He offers the subtitle of *ejercicio narrativo* (narrative exercise) to the novel *D*, which relates, in a most general sense, a history of the modernization of Venezuela as told through the development of radio and television. But this story evolves primarily through cassette tapes transcribed to form the major portion of the text. *Percusión* and *Medianoche en video: 1/5* are continuations of Balza's postmodern fictional project. *Percusión* relates a story that would not sound postmodern at all. But the transitional and provisional nature of all its settings and the protagonist's constant sense of metamorphosis, as well as his unstable identity, are all factors that relate this novel to many other Latin American postmodern fictions.

Alejandro Rossi, Francisco Massiani, Humberto Mata, Carlos Noguera, and Angel Gustavo Infante have also written some postmodern fictions in Venezuela. Their work, along with the postmodern fiction of Balza, affirm a certain presence of postmodern culture in Venezuela.

# Conclusion

Postmodern fiction obviously has made more inroads in some regions of South America than others. It tends to be most intensely cultivated in the largest cities—Buenos Aires, São Paulo, Santiago,

Bogotá, and Caracas. In the Andean region, perhaps more than any other, the postmodern novel is an expression of an exhausted truth. No viable character in the postmodern fiction of Moreno-Durán, Angel, Balza, Adoum, or Vargas Llosa can be a convincing voice of any truth. Rather, an attitude of exhaustion pervades the respective novelistic worlds of these characters. The postmodern reader of Andean, Brazilian, and Southern Cone fiction discovers that the postmodern novel in South America is frequently more political than might appear to be the case on the basis of a more superficial first reading. Obviously, postmodern fiction is a significant literary manifestation of the postmodern culture of the South American region.[17]

# 15

# *Postmodern Fiction in Mexico and the Caribbean*

## Introduction

Writers in Mexico City, Puerto Rico, and in exile from Cuba have produced a substantial volume of postmodern fiction. The Mexican postmodern scene from the mid-1960s to the 1990s has been one of the most active and vital in Latin America. The Caribbean, on the other hand, is defined by the same heterogeneity that has become a key word for the postmodern. In addition, social scientists have described the cultural constants of the Caribbean as fragmentation, instability, isolation, uprootedness, cultural complexity, disperse historiography, contingency, and impermanence. Several of these cultural constants are also closely related to concepts used to describe postmodern culture.

Postmodern cultures of the Caribbean, like that of Mexico, have been considerably impacted by both the mass culture and the high culture of the United States, and generally more so than is the case in South America. The Puerto Ricans, like the Mexicans, have been watching American television since the 1950s, and numerous bookstores in San Juan cater to readers of both Spanish and English; although, nowadays, the volumes in bookstores are being replaced, as they are in Mexico, by videos.

## Mexico

By 1967, signs of postmodern fiction were evident in Mexico, with the publication of three experimental and historical novels in that year: José Emilio Pacheco's *You Will Die in a Distant Land*, Carlos Fuentes's *Holy Place* and his *A Change of Skin*. The three works have some of the epistemological qualities of modernist fiction and some of the ontological qualities of postmodern writing. A such, they represent a transitional period in Mexican fiction.

The postmodern qualities of *You Will Die in a Distant Land* betray and subvert the unity suggested in an initial reading of this book as a harmonious modernist text. The subversion of the situation of two supposed characters named Eme and Someone does much more than undermine the reader's confidence in their existence. By questioning these narrative segments, *You Will Die in a Distant Land* questions the very possibility of writing history, the uses of history, and the legitimacy of historiography.

The boundaries between worlds are blurred and violated in *You Will Die in a Distant Land*. Pacheco shares the ontological concerns of postmodernism when he blurs the boundaries between the ancient and the modern worlds, as well as between the fascist operations of the Nazis and the "democratic" operations of more democratic states, such as Mexico. He also blurs the traditional distinction between story and history; his novel becomes an ontological text questioning its own mode of existence. The reader questions whether it exists as testimony, historiography, or fiction. Avoiding the either/or thinking of the Western tradition, Pacheco's text is a testimonial that subverts the testimonial itself, a historiography that questions historiography itself, and a metafiction that questions the mode of existence of fiction.

Fuentes's *Holy Place* and *A Change of Skin* share many postmodern qualities with *You Will Die in a Distant Land*. The title of Pacheco's novel refers to an "other" space: a woman in Leipzig reads Eme's palm and tells him, "You will die in a distant land." In this novel, as in the two works by Fuentes, the space of the novel is the territory of the other. The "holy place" in *Holy Place* is a sacred and personal space that, initially, is "far from the space of my mother, in the other side of the city." Later, the narrator-protagonist, who occupies various urban spaces from Mexico City to Rome, and from Paris to Orvieto, asks, "Is there another place?" (the postmodern question par excellence with respect to space). Later, he expresses the desire to be, as he says in English, "out of bounds." Space in *Holy Place*, like the characters, is in constant transformation—a constant rearranging of boundaries. The narrator states at one point, "nothing develops, everything is transfigured." Indeed, characters, like space, are in a constant state of transformation, emphasizing their indeterminate and unfixed quality. The protagonist himself, the 29-year-old Guillermo Nervo, suffers an identity crisis under the shadow of a dominant mother, a film celebrity. He finds no resolution to this crisis but, rather, speaks of his "other being." In the end, Guillermo reaches a state of exhaustion comparable to the exhausted states of the characters and implied reader in *You Will Die in a Distant Land*.

The four main characters of *A Change of Skin* are burned out too. Like *You Will Die in a Distant Land*, *A Change of Skin* is a historiographical metafiction and a novel in which characters have no fixed identity. Set in Mexico in the 1960s, *A Change of Skin* relates the story of two couples who spend a weekend together in Cholula, although there are numerous digressions into past history and other continents, including the Nazi period depicted in *You Will Die in a Distant Land*.

*A Change of Skin* is one of Fuentes's early experiments with characters having multiple (rather than just double) identities, as well as with characters and spaces in constant transformation. When it is ultimately revealed that the text of *A Change of Skin* has been produced by an inmate of an insane asylum, it is apparent that Fuentes's fiction has moved from concerns over the epistemological (evident in his novels of the early 1960s) to the ontological.

The transitional postmodern period of Mexico closes with the massacre of Tlatelolco in 1968 (the final outcome of a conflict between soldiers and protesters) and two experimental novels, José Agustín's *Inventando que sueño* (Inventing that I dream) and Elizondo's *El hipogeo secreto* (The secret cave). Both are so experimental, in fact, that many readers in the late 1960s were unsure if they should even be identified as novels. *Inventando que sueño* consists of a set of stories that can be read as separate stories or as a novel. It functions like an album of rock music containing several songs, and rock music is one of the predominant themes of the book.

After the hyperexperimentation of the late 1960s that culminated in the fiction of Pacheco, Fuentes, Agustín, and Elizondo, post-1968 postmodern fiction in Mexico became progressively less hermetic and more accessible. Nevertheless, postmodern attitudes of the 1960s became more acute, leading to a metafictional literature of exhaustion by the late 1980s. In addition to the work of such internationally recognized writers as Fuentes, the later postmodern writers in Mexico have included novelists such as Luis Arturo Ramos, María Luisa Puga, Brianda Domecq, Carmen Boullosa, and Ignacio Solares.

Like much postmodern fiction, *Terra Nostra* is strongly historical and political. Fuentes's awareness of historical discourse and, above all, his questioning of the very assumptions of Western historiography align *Terra Nostra* with the postmodern described by Linda Hutcheon. In this sense, *Terra Nostra* is more deeply historical and political than many modernist novels, including such overtly historical and political Latin American novels as García Márquez's *One Hundred Years of Solitude* and Vargas Llosa's *Conversation in The Cathedral.*

As a postmodern text, *Terra Nostra* is Fuentes's rewriting of the medieval, renaissance, and neoclassical architecture of El Escorial (the novel's setting). For Charles Jencks, one common postmodern architectural design is the skyscraper with perfectly modern lines, but also with classical Greek columns that place it in open opposition to modern design.[1] In this postmodern construct, no harmonic resolution of these blatantly contradictory lines is designed or desired. They remain in unresolved (postmodern) contradiction. The palace and other aspects of *Terra Nostra* function in this fashion. In his use of a "painting from Orvieto" (a mural by Luca Signorelli located in Orvieto, Italy), Fuentes appropriates this erotic mural and places it into El Señor's severe and austere palace. Just as the postmodern architect leaves the Greek columns on the modern building with no resolution, Fuentes leaves the Signorelli mural in the palace in open contradiction—with no visible resolution.

Some postmodern fiction in Mexico, while still more innovative than its modern predecessors, is far more accessible than early postmodern work. Luis Arturo Ramos, María Luisa Puga, Brianda Domecq, Carmen Boullosa, and Ignacio Solares are postmodern writers of this type. Ramos, Boullosa, and Solares tell stories with clearly defined plots but, like the Fuentes of *Distant Relations* and *Old Gringo,* they engage the reader in subtle games and devices associated with the postmodern. Ramos's early writing, particularly his short fiction, had clear affinities with Cortázar, and his story "Cartas para Julia" (Letters for Julia) contains the paranoia typical of some postmodern fiction (see chapter 14). His most accomplished and patently postmodern novel, *Este era un gato* (1987, This was a cat), tells the story of Roger Copeland, a retired American Marine captain who had participated in the 1914 invasion of Veracruz. Copeland returns to Mexico 60 years later, where he dies on exactly the same date he fought there in 1914, April 21. This novel deals with the otherness and the fragile identities that characterize Fuentes's fiction of the 1980s. Like much postmodern historiographic metafiction, *Este era un gato* does not fall into either "presentism" or nostalgia in its relation to the past that it represents. It does denaturalize that temporal relationship. The text offers three possible conclusions but ends in unresolved contradiction.

María Luisa Puga and Brianda Domecq have written a substantive body of postmodern fiction. Puga has published *Las posibilidades del odio* (1978, The possibilities of hatred), *Cuando el aire es azul* (1980, When the air is blue), *Pánico o peligro* (1981, Panic or danger), *La forma del silencio* (1987, The form of silence), *Antonia* (1989, Antonia). *Las posibilidades del odio* and *Cuando el aire es azul* are fundamentally modernist texts, but Puga's later work shows more postmodern impulses. Puga's fiction is often in the process of coming into being as it relates a story. *Pánico o peligro* is a metafiction that, like Fuentes's *Distant Relations*, suggests that narrating and living are basically the same activity, and that pictures characters with unstable identities. In *Pánico o peligro*, fictionalizing a story is a method for understanding the self. *La forma del silencio* is a more self-conscious meditation on the novel, suggesting that reality constructs the novel and the novel constructs reality. Puga's focus on words in particular contributes to this work's metafictional quality, and the use of an enigmatic style once again blurs the boundaries between traditional genres. A historiographic metafiction, *Antonia* relates the story of a Mexican woman who goes to London in search of traces of Virginia Woolf but confronts an identity crisis. Brianda Domecq has published two novels of interest within the context of the postmodern, the innovative works *La insólita historia de la Santa Cabora* (1990, The strange story of Saint Cabora) and *Once días ... y algo más* (1991, Eleven days ... and more).

Carmen Boullosa and Ignacio Solares have written recent fictions that are significant contributions to the Mexican postmodern novel. Solares had already established well-defined interests in both history and invention in his novels *Puerta al cielo* (1976, Door to the sky), *Anónimo* (1979, Anonymous), *El árbol del deseo* (1980, The tree of desire), *La fórmula de la inmortalidad* (1982, The formula for immortality), *Serafín* (1985, Seraphim), *Casas de encantamiento* (1988, Charmed houses), *Madero, el otro* (1989, Madero, the other), and *El gran elector* (1993, The great elector). *El gran elector* is a novel about a Mexican president who represents a composite of all the Mexican presidents of the PRI since 1930. (Speeches from numerous former presidents become the speeches of this fictionalized character.) The most predominant sign of the postmodern approach in *El gran elector* is the fact that everything, in the end, is discourse—different levels of speech—including the nation.

*La milagrosa* (1993, The miraculous one) is Boullosa's fourth novel in a body of work with several postmodern qualities. Her first novel, *Mejor desaparece* (1987, Better to disappear), contains the subjective *mirada* (gaze) of Fuentes's and Ramos's fiction. A historiographic metafiction set in the seventeenth century, Boullosa's *They're Cows, We're Pigs* (1991) espouses a postmodern ideology of plurality and recognition of difference. In *La milagrosa*, Boullosa tells the story of a religious faith healer; the novel seems to be symptomatic of a nation and of a fiction that is not truly irrational but that, paradoxically, involves a search for understanding things beyond the rational.

Both *El gran elector* and *La milagrosa* are critiques of political practices in postmodern Mexico. They represent the crisis of authority in Mexican society, the crisis of a world with little transcendence and little truth. Both novels contain a multiplicity of differing discourses—popular, political, ecclesiastical—in unresolved contradiction. The novels' concerns are predominantly ontological in a world with characters suffering identity crises.

Strongly affected by Borges, Cortázar, and North American writers, Mexican postmodern fiction of the late 1960s and 1970s entered a period of hyperexperimentation, a tendency headed by the Fuentes of *Birthday* and *Terra Nostra*, the Pacheco of *You Will Die in a Distant Land*, and the Elizondo of *Farabeuf* and *El hipogeo secreto*. The interests of these writers were generally more ontological than epistemological, with characters suffering from a lack of psychic unity, fragmentation, and unstable identity. The Mexican postmodern writers of the 1980s and 1990s have continued many of these tendencies, as well as other postmodern topics and devices, such as double coding, in fictions that are generally less technically experimental and accessible.

More recent Mexican postmodern writers have been less aggressively innovative in technique. Ramos, Solares, and Boullosa use narrative strategies associated with modernist fiction (fragmentation, multiple narrators, high levels of ambiguity, and so on), but they also develop their narratives using some of the proposals of Cortázar in *Hopscotch*. Like Pacheco, nevertheless, they require the active postmodern reader proposed by Morelli in *Hopscotch*. Ramos has also written occasional short fiction that one critic has defined as the "paranoic tale," which is present throughout Latin America among postmodern writers.[2]

# Puerto Rico

Puerto Rico has not been a stronghold of postmodern innovation, but Luis Rafael Sánchez has brought postmodern fiction to the forefront of Puerto Rican culture with the publication of *Macho Camacho's Beat* in 1976. He proceeded with his postmodern project with a second novel, *La importancia de llamarse Daniel Santos* (1988, The importance of calling oneself Daniel Santos). After the breakdown of the frontiers between popular and high culture already effected by Guillermo Cabrera Infante and Severo Sarduy in Cuba (as well as Manuel Puig in Argentina), Sánchez's novelization of the popular culture of Caribbean music and American television in *Macho Camacho's Beat* was a logical step in the Caribbean postmodern movement. As Carlos J. Alonso has indicated, *Macho Camacho's Beat* was, indeed, a turning point for Puerto Rican cultural production.[3] This novel represents a postmodern turn from earlier canonical works, such as Antonio S. Pedreira's *Insularismo* (Isolationism) Luis Palés Matos's statements on Afro-Antillean culture, René Marqués's seminal essays, and the gamut of solemn pronouncements on Puerto Rican cultural specificity.

The *guaracha* in the title of Sánchez's novel in the original Spanish, *La guaracha del Macho Camacho*, refers to the Puerto Rican music that permeates the text. Then, the author's epigraph is a refrain from the song "La guaracha del Macho Camacho," which states "Life is a phenomenal thing frontwards or backwards, however you swing." In his one-paragraph preface to the reader, Sánchez states that this novel is about the success of this song as well as the miserable and splendid extremes of life. At the end of the novel, he includes an appendix with the words to the song. The pages between these musical referents present a heterogeneous and fragmented text with multiple narrators who offer the popular music, mass culture, and heterogeneous cultural reality of everyday life in Puerto Rico, highlighted by an enormous traffic jam and the presence of Puerto Rican television star Iris Chacón.

Sánchez appropriates a multiplicity of discourses in this novel, including the voices of a radio announcer who appears in 19 segments, television and radio commercials, popular singers, and many other voices of the mass media. Sánchez also parodies writers associated with high culture, reproducing the African rhythm and sounds of poets such as Palés Matos. Latin American writers such as Donoso and Sarduy are also suggested in the text. The author makes allusions to a broad range of cultural figures and objects, including Frankenstein, Mohammad Ali, "From the Halls of Montezuma," Eugenio María de Hostos, George Wallace, Fidel Castro, Mao, "Over the Hills," John Wayne, the Green Berets, Marcel Schwob, García Lorca's *Romancero gitano*, Charlie Chaplin, and Cantinflas.

*Macho Camacho's Beat* is a double-coded novel whose parodic humor seems to celebrate popular culture and such popular culture figures as Iris Chacón. Indeed, it can be read as a burlesque celebration of humor and music—as an upbeat experience that moves constantly to the rhythm of Macho Camacho. The other side of Sánchez's double-coded book, however, invites the postmodern reader to interpret it as a critique of Puerto Rico's colonial status and the function of American mass media in such a society. Similarly, it is an indictment of the language of American advertising in Third World countries, while inviting the active postmodern reader to observe a variety of passive receivers of radio and television messages.

Sánchez's *La importancia de llamarse Daniel Santos* is a more overtly postmodern text dealing with an author's search for the story of Daniel Santos, the popular Puerto Rican singer of the 1940s and 1950s . The author figure, who is identified in the text as a gay writer named Luis Rafael Sánchez, travels from Puerto Rico to such places as Guayquil, Caracas, Cali, Quito, Barranquilla, Managua, and Bogotá in search of the complete story of Santos, who had sung in those cities. Sánchez escapes generic definitions, as his book blurs the boundaries between fiction, biography, and testimonial writing. The author describes his text in the early stages as a hybrid, frontier, and mestizo narration, exempt from generic regulations. Near the end of the text, he also overtly recognizes his debts to his modernist predecessor Alejo Carpentier and his postmodern predecessor Severo Sarduy.

This novel is a self-conscious analysis of myths. Many of Sánchez's traditional and modernist predecessors in Latin America created myths, and some of his modernist predecessors debunked myths. In *La importancia de llamarse Daniel Santos*, Sánchez neither creates nor debunks the myths surrounding the figure of Daniel Santos, but questions how popular figures such as he are mythicized and demythicized.

After Sánchez, the only other notable figure on the postmodern literary scene in Puerto Rico is Edgardo Rodríguez Juliá, author of two novel-like books that escape traditional genre definition, *La noche oscura del niño Avilés* (1984, The dark night of the Avilés boy), and *Una noche con Iris Chacón* (1986, A night with Iris Chacón).

Postmodern fiction in Puerto Rico often straddles the unstable and indeterminate cultural boundaries between the United States and Latin America. The Puerto Rican writers' leap to the ontological is often based on an awareness of the epistemological limits of writing in a society dominated by American culture.

# Cuba

The early signs of a nascent postmodern culture in Cuba was signaled by one seminal book, *Three Trapped Tigers* (1967) by Guillermo Cabrera Infante. An initial indicator that Cabrera Infante belongs in the postmodern arena is his obvious affiliation with James Joyce, primarily because of his treatment of language itself as a subject of this novel. Cabrera Infante's tone, however, is of skeptical nostalgia, which has nothing to do with Joyce.[4]

*Three Trapped Tigers* is a fragmented, open novel in constant postmodern movement and transformation. Set in the 1958 Cuba that was enjoying the music of Benny Moré and the acting of Veronica Lake, this novel communicates a sense of the end of an era and of finality. Like many postmodern novels, the main subject of *Three Trapped Tigers* is language itself, making it an important predecessor to the postmodern novel in Cuba and Latin America.

The work of Severo Sarduy differs considerably from Cabrera Infante's, but it is one of the most significant contributions to the Caribbean postmodern movement. Sarduy's novel with the most impact on the Latin American postmodern novel in general is *Cobra* (1972). This work consists of two interwoven narratives, the first of which, the "Teatro Lírico de Muñecas" (Lyrical Theater of Dolls), takes place in a burlesque house. The protagonist is Cobra, a transsexual star at the theater. Cobra and the owner of the theater, La Señora, attempt to reduce the size of Cobra's feet, but the drug they take reduces the pair to dwarfs named Pup and La Señorita. Then Cobra goes to India in search of the proper oriental paints and colors for the theater. In the other narrative, Cobra goes to Tangiers in search of a doctor famous for sex-change operations, Dr. Ktazob; Cobra is directed to him by drug pushers from Amsterdam. The novel concludes in the snow at the Chinese-Tibet border, where Cobra has gone with a motorcycle gang.

Written more under the hermetic sign of Lezama Lima than with the playful chaos of Cabrera Infante, *Cobra* is Sarduy's novelistic reflection on language and writing. In this novel, language is not just a means of communication but a way of demonstrating the function of language. The novel's title refers to a poem by Octavio Paz from *Conjunciones y disyunciones* that dramatizes the generation of language. The association of words in this poem creates more words, a process parallel to much of *Cobra*.

The characters in *Cobra*, rather than attempting to portray "real" characters of fiction, represent only representation. The characters Cobra and Cadillac also project the artificial sexuality of their respective genders, and Cadillac represents excessive machismo. Their speech is artificial, obviously consisting of a variety of discourses that show the distance of the language from its origins. Consequently, the postmodern characters in *Cobra* question the representation of the subject in traditional and modern fiction.

*Cobra* was one of the early texts of Caribbean and Latin American postmodern fiction to blur the line between fictional and theoretical discourse. The two stages of the journal *Tel Quel* reflect the changing interests of Sarduy; and the second stage of the journal (1964–1970), dominated by the thinking of Jacques Derrida and Jacques Lacan, relate most directly to this novel. These two theorists place into question the concept of the subject as unifying element; the play of infinite substitutions, according to Derrida, frees language from the need for "unity" or "meaning." In *Cobra*, Sarduy uses such playful substitutions to carry out his parody of Derrida. The confluence of theory and practice in the novel produces not an essence, but a lack of essence, thus pointing to the privileging of artificiality and superficiality in the novel.

*Cobra* is also a work of ongoing double coding, with subjects who are and are not "real" characters, which tell stories that the work then proceeds to negate. In the process of constant transmutation, Cobra is male, female, and transvestite, a castrato and, inexplicably, a square root itself. This novel also contains the double coding of parody as well as the double coding of fictional and theoretical discourse. These double codings question the literary hierarchies of modernist practices and challenge the active postmodern reader to confront the gaps produced by this ontological inquiry.

Sarduy's novels *Maitreya* (1978, Matreya) and *Colibrí* (1983, Hummingbird) represent a continuation of the author's postmodern project. Like Cobra, the protagonist in these two novels are subjects-in-progress. La Tremenda in *Maitreya* is also identified as la Expansiva, la Divina, la Colonial, la Masiva, la Toda-Mena, and la Delirium. The characters travel through India to Ceylon, and from there to Cuba. *Maitreya* offers some of the hermetic qualities of the postmodern fiction of Piglia, Eltit, and Fuentes, all of whom have been affected by Sarduy's postmodern fiction of the 1970s.

The uncertain and unstable identities of the narrator and the protagonist are the most clearly postmodern aspects of *Colibrí*. The novel opens with the image of the protagonist dancing nude between two mirrors, behind a bar, and the mirrors multiply Colibrí's image ad infinitum. This multiplicity is played out in the remainder of the novel, from Colibrí's unknown origins to his amorphous character. The narrator, who seems to be an author figure, assumes both masculine and feminine guises.

Like Eltit, Piglia, and the Fuentes of *Terra Nostra*, Sarduy returns to the very roots of Latin American culture, deconstructing its most basic elements, beginning with language. In his later novel *Cocoyo* (1990), Sarduy continues his postmodern project, novelizing many of the concerns already seen in *Maitreya* and *Colibrí*.

The most notable Cuban exponents of postmodern fiction are Cabrera Infante and Sarduy. A culture as inherently postmodern as Cuba's has produced several other writers with postmodern tendencies, including Reinaldo Arenas, Senel Paz, and René Vásquez Díaz.

# Dominican Republic

In the 1940s and 1950s, after the rise of a Creole poetry and the modern poetry called Independent in the Dominican Republic, poets associated with La Poesía Sorprendida (surprised poetry) contributed to the modernization of literature. The most prominent modernist fiction writers of the Dominican Republic have been Aída Cartagena Portolatín, Marcio Veloz Maggiolo, Pedro Mir, and Pedro Verges.

The Dominican Republic certainly is not a center of postmodern fictional production in the Caribbean or the Americas. Nevertheless, Marcio Veloz Maggiolo, Efraín Castillo, Andrés L. Mateo, and Manuel García Cartagena do show some affinities with postmodernism. Veloz Maggiolo demonstrated interests in the postmodern with experiments such as *Florbella* (1986, Florbella),and *Materia Prima* (1988, Raw material). Neither of these novels is as experimental as their daring subtitles suggest, but they reveal Veloz Maggiolo's postmodern attitudes. In his two novels, Efraím Castillo novelizes issues of American and Dominican culture. Andrés L. Mateo attempts experiments with language and chapter structure in *Pisar los dedos de Dios* (1979, Stepping on the fingers of God) and *La otra Penélope* (1982, The other Penelope), both of which deal with the subjective state of the characters in an urban setting. The young writer Manuel García Cartagena's first novel, *Aquiles Vargas, fantasma* (1989, Aquiles Vargas, phantom), is a self-conscious metafiction that questions the political future of the Dominican Republic as well as the status of his book as a novel.

# Conclusion

Innovative and experimental fiction has been amply developed in Mexico and the Caribbean since the rise of the modernist writers of the 1940s and 1950s—Agustín Yáñez, Juan Rulfo, Carlos Fuentes, and Alejo Carpentier. They were the producers of the grand narrative, memorable characters, and their interests were fundamentally epistemological. Since the late 1960s, Mexican and Caribbean fiction has undergone a radical transformation in the direction of postmodern experimentation.

Postmodern culture in the Caribbean is one of the most heterogeneous of Latin America because of the multiple language and culture groups that coexist in close geographic proximity. In addition, the acutely hierarchical class structure in much of the Caribbean and its proximity to the United States contribute to the special heterogeneity of the Caribbean.

The postmodern novelists of Mexico and the Caribbean write
with a full awareness of the provisional and precarious status of
their respective cultures in close interaction with American culture,
and often dominated by it. Truth is as unstable, provisional, and
fluid in the texts of these Caribbean postmodern writers as are many
other features of this writing. Truth is as ambiguous as many of the
characters themselves, who tend to speak in the formulaic patterns
imposed on them by foreign and national mass media and popular
culture.

# 16

# *Conclusions: Toward a Modern, Postmodern, and Postnational Novel*

Writing in the mid-1960s, Octavio Paz claimed that since the nineteenth century the Latin American writer has always desired to be modern: "modernity has been our style for a century. It's the universal style. To want to be modern seems crazy: we are condemned to be modern, since we are prohibited from the past and the future."[1] Indeed, several generations of Latin American writers since the late nineteenth century have insisted on being part of the ongoing Western desire to be modern.

Before Asturias and Carpentier, there were two generations of Latin American writers who desired to be modern—the turn-of-the-century *modernistas* and the *vanguardistas* of the 1920s. With Asturias, Yáñez, Marechal, and Carpentier, the Latin American writers still desired to be modern, finding ways to use the aesthetics of modernism to express their own vision of reality. This was the third moment that Latin American writers wanted to be modern. They and the Brazilian novelists of the northeast found their basic method by exercising the right of invention and practicing a new type of Faulknerian regionalism—transcendent regionalism.

The writers of the Boom fervently desired to be modern and pursued the modernist project of their forefathers with absolute confidence, producing some of the major novels of the Spanish language in the process. As such, they were the fourth generation that wanted to be modern. After struggling in their early years to finally affirm their modernity, each of these writers took on the charge of composing their respective "total" novel—represented by such totalizing modernist projects as *One Hundred Years of Solitude* and *Conversation in The Cathedral*.

The next generation—the fifth moment—that has sought to be modern is the postmodern writers, who have seemed less ambitious than the authors of those "total" novels. They have rejected the totalizing projects of their forefathers and looked to international postmodern culture in literature, film, and theory for their modernity. They have tended to reject the role of public intellectual assumed by the writers of the Boom yet, at the same time, find new political discourses in their writing.

This new modernity called postmodernism has involved a new cultural and political force in Latin American writing of the 1980s and 1990s: feminism. Indeed, the rise of women writers and articulation of feminist politics have been major phenomena since the 1980s. The recent popularity of Isabel Allende and Laura Esquivel, in conjunction with the general international interest in both Latin American writing and women's writing, has placed women writers in Latin America in the spotlight for the first time in the history of the region. Of course, women have been writing in Latin America since the colonial period, with Sor Juan Inés de la Cruz being the most prominent example. Several women writers are producing an innovative postmodern fiction in Latin America, such as Carmen Boullosa, Albalucía Angel, Diamela Eltit, Cristina Peri Rossi, and Sylvia Molloy.

For Jean Franco, a well-informed British critic and scholar practicing in U.S. academia, feminist theory fails as a theory if it does not change the study of literature substantially.[2] Latin American feminist theory, according to Franco, must use as a point of departure a critique of institutions and, above all, the literary system itself. This feminist theory need not begin from zero because its interests touch those of other intellectual tendencies, particularly those of deconstruction, semiotics, and Marxist theories of ideology. Deconstructionist criticism, as Franco points out, contributes to feminist analysis because it shows how rooted binary thinking is in Western thought and the oppositions that it produces. (Interestingly enough, this binary thinking was a matter of constant critique by Fuentes and Cortázar in the 1960s.) Franco also points out that we are now entering into a postmodern period of the end of the master narratives—the global and totalizing theories that were always based on the exclusion of the heterogeneous. Today, it is relatively easy to deconstruct binary systems of colonial or nationalist thought. But Franco concludes that pluralism also has its risks: if everything is valid, then nothing is valid.

The new feminist fiction of Latin America is characterized by daring attitudes toward literary discourse and a direct questioning of dominant ideologies. Many of the Latin American women writers of the 1980s, Angel, Eltit, Susana Torres Molina, and Helena Parente Cunha included, are not only aware of their roles as women writers in Latin America but also are fully conscious of feminist theory. For the first time in Latin American fiction, the unmasking of ideology and an analysis of the social construction of gender are carried out with a self-conscious and overt understanding of ideology and feminist theory. For example, many of these women seek to understand social and cultural practices in order to clarify how gender relations are constituted, reproduced, and contested. Most of these feminist writers seek an understanding, in different ways, of gender under patriarchal capitalist regimes. Angel, Eltit, Parente Cunha, and others share poststructuralist interests in the theory of language, subjectivity, and power as knowledge production. Many of these writers have also been engaged in a search for an *écriture feminine.*

Feminists such as the Argentine Torres Molina and the Puerto Rican Rosario Ferré have agendas similar to those of cultural feminists in the United States.[3] Torres Molina is not as formally innovative as Angel and Eltit, but Torres Molina's set of stories *Dueña y señora* (1983, Owner and lady) represented a major breakthrough in contemporary Argentine writing when it began to circulate in Buenos Aires. The lesbian encounters in this book scandalized Argentina's conservative reading public. Never before had an Argentine woman celebrated the female body and lesbianism in such a fashion.

Ferré has written a large volume of fiction and essays dealing with the marginalization of women and racial prejudice in Puerto Rico. In her novel *Maldito amor* (1986, Damn love), she relates how several marginalized sectors of society revise and appropriate the history of Puerto Rico. In addition to the marginality of women and racial prejudice, Ferré's writing often focuses on female creativity, frequently by means of sexual language.

The Brazilian Helena Parente Cunha, a professor of literary theory at the Universidade Federal in Rio de Janeiro, published her first novel, *Women between Mirrors* (originally written in Portuguese), in 1983. Given her background in literary theory, Parente Cunha is more similar to Angel and Eltit in some ways than to Torres Molina. Previously unknown as a fiction writer in Brazil, Parente Cunha in this work demonstrates interest in psychoanalytic models of sexuality and subjectivity. *Women between Mirrors* is an experiment in privileging the subjective in constituting the meaning of a middle-aged woman's lived reality. The protagonist is a 45-year-old Brazilian married to an extraordinarily dominant Brazilian man. She also has three teenage sons. The narrative is her response to the otherness of female sexuality that has been repressed.

In this novel, the act of writing functions as a paradigm of power relationships. The protagonist struggles with "the woman who writes me" just as she struggles with her husband. She gradually takes control of her entire situation, exercising power over both the woman who writes her and her husband. *Women between Mirrors* is a heterogeneous and theoretically self-conscious work that is typical of some of the most engaging feminist novels written in Latin America in the 1980s.

In many ways, the postmodern feminist writers of the 1980s and 1990s have taken over the political agenda of the Latin American writers of the Boom in the 1960s. The binary thinking that Fuentes and Cortázar criticized so severely in the 1960s has become central to the agenda of these postmodern women writers. At the same time, much recent feminist, gay, and lesbian writing shares the multiple political agenda of postmodern writers such as Fuentes, Piglia, and Pacheco.

The latest trends in postmodern fiction and the new feminist agenda represent a sixth moment of writers wanting to be modern. In the latest moment, postmodern and feminist writers are expressing a postnationalist world view. They see themselves participating in an international agenda in which they share aesthetic and political commonalities with writers throughout the Americas and Europe. By the end of the century, the modernity of the Latin American writer has been well established. Binary thought has been questioned and rejected by two generations of these writers. Traditionalism and nationalism in culture and politics have become attitudes of the past, for the predominant mind-set among Latin American novelists at the end of the century is postnationalist.

# Notes and References

## CHAPTER 1

1. The predominant mode of writing fiction prior to the rise of the modernist novel in the 1940s was a traditional realist-modernist fiction with themes related to *criollismo*—a search for national identity by exalting local values, particularly the special qualities of the land. For further introduction to this fiction and *criollismo*, see John S. Brushwood, *The Spanish-American Novel: A Twentieth-Century Survey* (Austin: University of Texas Press, 1966); Naomi Lindstrom, *Twentieth-Century Spanish American Fiction* (Austin: University of Texas Press, 1994); Gerald Martin, *Journeys through the Labyrinth: Latin American Fiction of the Twentieth Century* (London: Verso, 1989).

2. I have discussed the role of individual consciousness in modernist fiction in more detail in Raymond Leslie Williams, *The Postmodern Novel in Latin America* (New York: St. Martin's, 1995), chapter 1.

3. Martin has clearly delineated the presence of Joyce in Latin America in several chapters of *Journeys through the Labyrinth.*

4. Brushwood discusses the right of invention and the role of Borges in *The Spanish American Novel.* See in particular chapters 11 and 12.

5. Brushwood cites the eminent Arturo Torres Rioseco, who, in the 1920s, claimed that avant-garde fiction was an "inappropriate form of expression." See *The Spanish American Novel,* 81–82.

6. For an in-depth discussion of these now-classic novels of the "land," see Carlos Alonso, *The Spanish-American Regionalist Novel: Modernity and Autochthony* (Cambridge: Cambridge University Press, 1990).

7. For an additional discussion of the role of Borges in postmodern fiction in Latin America, see Williams, *The Postmodern Novel in Latin America,* chapter 1.

8. Brushwood discusses transcendent regionalism in the Spanish American novel in *The Spanish American Novel.* He uses this concept in several chapters relating to the rise of modernist fiction after 1945.

9. For a lengthy discussion of the four major regionalist novelists in Brazil, see Fred Ellison, *Brazil's New Novel* (Berkeley: University of California Press, 1954).

## CHAPTER 2

1. Brushwood, *The Spanish American Novel,* 161.
2. Ibid.
3. Lindstrom, *Twentieth-Century Spanish American Fiction,* 100.
4. Richard Callan, *Miguel Angel Asturias* (Boston: Twayne, 1970), 33–34.
5. Ibid., 34.
6. George McMurray, *Spanish American Writing since 1941* (New York: Ungar, 1987), 21.

7. Callan, *Miguel Angel Asturias*, 54.

8. Lindstrom, *Twentieth-Century Spanish American Fiction*, 100.

9. Martin, *Journeys through the Labyrinth*, 174.

10. Ibid., 178.

11. Callan, *Miguel Angel Asturias*, 70.

12. Ibid., 84.

13. Walter Ong, *Orality and Literacy: The Technologizing of the Word* (London: Methuen, 1982); see chapter 2.

14. Lindstrom, *Twentieth-Century Spanish American Fiction*, 102.

15. Brushwood, *The Spanish American Novel*, 188.

16. Callan, *Miguel Angel Asturias*, 107–9.

17. Numerous critics have made reference to topics such as reality, fantasy, and magic in the work of Asturias; see Helmy F. Giacoman, *Homenaje a Miguel Angel Asturias* (New York: Las Americas Publishing, 1971).

## CHAPTER 3

1. John S. Brushwood, *Mexico in Its Novel* (Austin: University of Texas Press, 1966), 10.

2. These vignettes of life in rural Jalisco appeared later in a single volume, Agustín Yáñez, *Los sentidos al aire* (Mexico City: Fondo de Cultura Económica, 1985). Yáñez published *Flor de juegos antiguos* in Mexico (Mexico City: Grijalbo, 1977); the original edition had appeared in 1942.

3. Joseph Sommers, *After the Storm: Landmarks of the Modern Mexican Novel* (Albuquerque: University of New Mexico Press, 1968), 42.

4. Ibid.

5. Ibid., 61.

6. Brushwood, *Mexico in Its Novel*, 165.

7. Ibid., 166.

8. Ibid., 167.

9. Ibid., 45.

10. José Luis Martínez, *Agustín Yáñez* (Guadalajara: Universidad de Guadalajara, 1984), 64.

11. John S. Brushwood, "La arquitectura de las novelas de Agustín Yáñez," in *Homenaje a Agustín Yáñez*, ed. Helmy F. Giacoman (New York: Las Américas Publishing, 1973), 95–116.

12. See John J. Flasher, *México contemporáneo en las novelas de Agustín Yáñez* (Mexico: Editorial Porrúa, 1969); see especially 151–74.

13. Ibid., 160.

14. Brushwood, "La arquitectura de las novelas de Agustín Yáñez," 108.

## CHAPTER 4

1. Raymond D. Souza, *Major Cuban Novelists* (Columbia: University of Missouri Press, 1976).

2. Roberto González Echevarría, *Alejo Carpentier: The Pilgrim at Home* (Ithaca, N.Y.: Cornell University Press, 1977), 15.

3. For more discussion on Fernando Ortiz and related intellectuals in Cuba, see ibid., 44–51.

4. Brushwood, *The Spanish American Novel*, 97–108.

5. Alejo Carpentier, *El reino de este mundo* (Havana: Bolsilibros Union, 1964), xiii.

6. Ibid., xv.

7. The term *magic realism* has been applied to a diverse group of writers and often in reference to any type of writing that portrayed both the empirical real and the fantastic. The German art critic Franz Roh first coined the term in 1925 as a magic insight into reality. For Roh, it was synonymous with postexpressionist painting (1920–1925) because it revealed the mysterious elements hidden in everyday reality. Magic realism expressed human astonishment before the wonders of the real world. The bibliography on this topic is lengthy; with respect to Latin American literature, see in particular Seymour Menton, *Magic Realism Rediscovered, 1918–1981* (Philadelphia: Art Alliance Press, 1983), and Lois Parkinson Zamora and Wendy B. Faris, eds., *Magical Realism: Theory, History, Community* (Durham, N.C.: Duke University Press, 1995).

8. González Echevarría, *Alejo Carpentier*, 98.

9. Ibid., 123.

10. Ong, *Orality and Literacy*, chapter 2.

11. Souza, *Major Cuban Novelists*, 39.

12. Ibid., 44

13. Ibid.

14. González Echevarría, *Alejo Carpentie*, 158.

15. Ibid.

16. Ibid., 159.

17. Ibid.

18. Ong, *Orality and Literacy*, chapter 2.

19. Carpentier, *El reino de este mundo*, 70.

20. Ong, *Orality and Literacy*, chapter 2.

21. González Echevarría, *Alejo Carpentier*, 191.

22. Hugo Rodríguez Alcalá, "Sentido de *El Camino de Santiago*," in *Asedios a Alejo Carpentier*, ed. Klaus Muller Bergh (Santiago: Editorial Universitaria, 1972), 165–77.

23. Roberto Gonález Echevarría, "*Semejante a la noche* de Alejo Carpentier," in Muller Bergh, *Asedios a Alejo Carpentier*, 178.

24. Ibid., 180.

25. Souza, *Major Cuban Novelists*, 45–46.

26. Ibid., 47.

27. Ibid., 49.

28. Roberto González Echevarría, *Celestina's Brood: Continuities of the Baroque in Spanish and Latin American Literature* (Durham, N.C.: Duke University Press, 1993), 142–43.

29. Ibid.

30. Ibid., 143.

31. In the 1970s, a series of novels on the dictator theme was published in Latin America. Among the most prominent of these were García

Márquez's *The Autumn of the Patriarch*, Roa Bastos's *I, the Supreme*, and Carpentier's *Reasons of State*.

32. Roberto González Echevarría, "Alejo Carpentier," in *Modern Latin American Fiction Writers*, vol. 113 of *Dictionary of Literary Biography* (Detroit: Gale Research Inc. 1992), 108.

33. Souza, *Major Cuban Novelists*, 51.

## CHAPTER 5

1. For a study of the cultural activities of the Martin Fierro group in Buenos Aires, see Vicky Unruh, *Latin American Vanguards: The Art of Contentious Encounters* (Berkeley: University of California Press, 1994).

2. Brushwood, *The Spanish American Novel*, 168.

3. Lindstrom, *Twentieth-Century Spanish American Fiction*, 106.

4. Brushwood, *The Spanish American Novel*, 168.

5. Ibid., 135.

6. Lindstrom, *Twentieth-Century Spanish American Fiction*, 144.

7. Ibid., 145.

8. Brushwood, *The Spanish American Novel*, 181.

9. Djelal Kadir, *Juan Carlos Onetti* (Boston: Twayne, 1977), 92.

10. Ibid., 94.

11. Ibid., 95.

12. Ibid., 98.

13. Ibid., 75.

14. Ibid., 76.

15. Ibid., 119.

## CHAPTER 6

1. Brushwood has described transcendent regionalism as the type of regionalism that surpasses local boundaries. See *The Spanish American Novel*, chapters 12 and 14.

2. Fred P. Ellison, *Brazil's New Novel* (Berkeley: University of California Press, 1954), 50.

3. Ibid.

4. Ibid., 59.

5. Bobby J. Chamberlain, *Jorge Amado* (Boston: Twayne, 1984).

6. Ellison, *Brazil's New Novel*, 132, n. 63.

7. Celso Lemos de Oliveira, *Understanding Graciliano Ramos* (Columbia: University of South Carolina Press, 1988), 47.

8. Richard A. Mazzara, *Graciliano Ramos* (New York: Twayne, 1974).

9. Ibid., 53.

10. Ibid., 54.

11. Ellison, *Brazil's New Novel*, 135.

## CHAPTER 7

1. José Donoso has discussed the development of the political positions of the writers of the Boom in his *Historia personal del Boom* (Barcelona: Anagrama, 1972).

2. Brushwood has discussed some of these common threads of Latin American fiction of the 1960s in *The Spanish American Novel*, 266–67.

3. A few Latin American writers were universally acclaimed and known throughout Latin America. Their fame had not spread instantaneously, however, as was the case with Vargas Llosa after the publication of *The Time of the Hero*. To the contrary, it took years and, in some cases decades, for these writers to gain an international readership.

4. I have discussed the politics of the writers of the Boom during this period in Raymond Leslie Williams, *The Writings of Carlos Fuentes* (Austin: University of Texas Press, 1996), 37.

## CHAPTER 8

1. For a discussion of Foucault and Fuentes, see Williams, *The Writings of Carlos Fuentes*, 44.

2. In *The Writings of Carlos Fuentes*, the appendix contains a lengthy interview I did with Fuentes in which we discuss the cycles of his fiction, as he has delineated them in "La Edad del Tiempo."

3. In my interview with Fuentes about his cycle, he discussed several novels that are planned but not yet written. For a brief discussion of what Fuentes said of *Los años con Laura Díaz*, see *The Writings of Carlos Fuentes*, 123.

4. I have a more expanded conclusion, making several of these same points, in *The Writings of Carlos Fuentes*.

## CHAPTER 9

1. Robert Brody has discussed the quest theme in *Hopscotch* at length in *Julio Cortázar: Rayuela* (London: Grant and Cutler, 1976); see especially chapter 1.

2. Lucille Kerr, *Reclaiming the Author: Figures and Fictions from Spanish America*, (Durham, N.C: Duke University Press, 1992), 26–45.

3. Ibid., 27.

4. Jonathan Tittler has entered into detailed analysis of the eroticism in *A Manual for Manuel* in *Narrative Irony in the Contemporary Spanish American Novel* (Ithaca, N.Y: Cornell University Press, 1984); see chapter 6.

5. See Ibid., 157.

## CHAPTER 10

1. José Miguel Oviedo has discussed the telescoping effect in *Conversation in The Cathedral* in *Mario Vargas Llosa: la invención de una realidad* (Barcelona: Seix Barral, 1970).

2. For evidence of Vargas Llosa's fascination with the story of Canudos, see Raymond Leslie Williams, *Mario Vargas Llosa* (New York: Ungar, 1977).

3. Some of the observations in this chapter were originally set forth in my *Mario Vargas Llosa*.

## CHAPTER 11

1. There is contradictory information available about García Márquez's birth date. Most scholars list his birth date in accordance with what the author himself claims—1928. There are other indicators that he was really born in 1927. In Colombia, a reliable source (a close personal friend of García Márquez) once showed me a photocopy of a birth document indicating that he was born in 1927. Even though I have listed his birth date as 1928 in several published pieces, I am now convinced that he was really born in 1927.

2. For an in-depth discussion of this extensive monologue and other features of narrative point of view, see Raymond Leslie Williams, *Gabriel García Márquez* (Boston: G. K. Hall, 1984), chapter 4.

3. Ong, *Orality and Literacy.*

4. Gabriel García Márquez, *One Hundred Years of Solitude*, trans. Gregory Rabassa (New York: Harper and Row, 1970), 27.

5. See Williams, *Gabriel García Márquez*, 111, for García Márquez's quoted explanation.

6. See ibid., 111, for fuller discussion of the theme of power.

7. García Márquez, *One Hundred Years of Solitude*, 115.

## CHAPTER 12

1. Brushwood has discussed the small-screen novel in *The Spanish American Novel*, chapter 15.

2. Raymond D. Souza, *The Poetic Fiction of José Lezama Lima* (Columbia: University of Missouri Press, 1983), 21.

3. For a further discussion of the contradictions between time and language, see ibid., 21–37.

## CHAPTER 13

1. Two recent books on the postmodern novel in Latin America are Santiago Colas, *Postmodernity in Latin America: The Argentine Paradigm* (Durham, N.C.: Duke University Press, 1994), and Williams, *The Postmodern Novel in Latin America.*

2. Linda Hutcheon, *A Poetics of Postmodernism: History, Theory, Fiction* (New York: Routledge, 1988), 36.

3. Jean-Francois Lyotard, *The Postmodern Condition: A Report on Knowledge*, vol. 10, *Theory and History of Literature* (Minneapolis: University of Minnesota Press, 1989), 37.

4. Jean Baudrillard, *Simulations* (New York: Semiotext(e), 1983), 31.

5. Ibid., p. 44.

6. Hutcheon, *A Poetics of Postmodernism*, 93.

7. Angela McCrobbie, *Postmodernism and Popular Culture* (New York: Routledge, 1994).

## CHAPTER 14

1. Lucille Kerr, *Reclaiming the Author*, 24.

2. Ellen McCracken, "Metaplagiarism and the Critics' Role as Detective: Ricardo Piglia's Reinvention of Roberto Arlt," *PMLA* 106, nos. 4–6 (1991): 1071–82.

3. Ibid.

4. See Sandra Garabano "Reescribiendo la nación: la narrativa de Ricardo Piglia," (Ph.D diss., University of Colorado, 1994) for a discussion of this matter.

5. See Magdalena García Pinto's interview with Molloy in *Historias íntimas: conversaciones con diez escritoras latinoamicanas* (Hanover, N.H.: Ediciones del Norte, 1988), 134.

6. Ibid., 135.

7. Clarice Lispector, *The Hour of the Star* (New York: Carcanet Press, 1986). The novel first appeared in Portuguese in 1977.

8. Robert E. DiAntonio points to the numerous directions of the contemporary Brazilian novel in *Brazilian Fiction: Aspects and Evolution of the Contemporary Narrative* (Fayetteville: University of Arkansas Press, 1989).

9. Ibid., 18.

10. Julio Ortega, "Diamela Eltit y el Imaginarioa de la Virtualidad," in *Una poética de literatura menor: la narrativa de Diamela Eltit,* ed. Juan Carlos Lértora (Santiago de Chile: Para Textos/Cuarto Propio, 1993), 53.

11. Sara Castro-Klarén, "La crítica literaria feminista y la escritora en América Latina," in *La sartan por el mango,* eds. Patricia González and Eliana Ortega (San Juan: Ediciones Huracán, 1985), 25–46.

12. Ortega, "Diamela Eltit y el Imaginario de la Virtualidad," 53.

13. Hutcheon, *A Poetics of Postmodernism,* 119.

14. Guillermo García Corales, "La deconstrucción del poder en *Lumpérica,* in Lértora, *Una poética de literatura menor,* 111.

15. Keith Booker, *Vargas Llosaa among the Postmodernists* (Gainesville: University Press of Florida, 1994).

16. Santiago Colas, "Un posmodernismo resistente: *El diez por ciento de la vida* y la historia," *Nuevo texto crítico* 7 (1991): 175–96.

17. I have discussed many of the issues of this chapter, as well as other postmodern writers from South America, in *The Postmodern Novel in Latin America.*

## CHAPTER 15

1. See Charles Jencks, *What Is Postmodernism?* (London: Academy Editions; New York: St. Martin's, 1986).

2. Garabano has discussed the paranoic tale in Latin America, as it pertains to the writing of Ricardo Piglia, in "Reescribiendo la nación: la narrativa de Ricardo Piglia."

3. Carlos J. Alonso, *"La guaracha del Macho Camacho:* The Novel as Dirge," *MLN* 100 (March 1985): 350.

4. Brushwood, *The Spanish American Novel,* 292.

## CHAPTER 16

1. Octavio Paz, *Poesía en movimiento: Mexico 1915–1966* (Mexico City: Siglo XXI Editores, 1966), 5.

2. Jean Franco, "Apuntes sobre la crítica feminista y la literatura hispanoamericana," *Hispamérica* 15 (December 1986): 31–43.

3. See Linda Alcoff, "Cultural Feminism versus Postructuralism: The Identity Crisis in Feminist Theory," *Signs: Journal of Women in Culture and Society* 13, no. 3 (1988): 405–36, in which she sets forth the concept of "cultural feminism."

# Selected Bibliography

Alcoff, Linda. "Cultural Feminism versus Postructuralism: The Identity Crisis in Feminist Theory." *Signs: Journal of Women in Culture and Society.* 13, no. 3 (1988): 405–36.

Alonso, Carlos. "*La guaracha del Macho Camacho:* The Novel as Dirge." *MLN* 100 (March 1985): 348–60.

———. *The Spanish American Regional Novel: Modernity and Autochthony.* Cambridge: Cambridge University Press, 1990.

Baudrillard, Jean. *Simulations.* New York: Semiotext(e), 1983.

Brody, Robert. *Julio Cortázar: Rayuela.* London: Grant and Cutler, 1976.

Brushwood, John S. *Mexico in its Novel.* Austin: University of Texas Press, 1966.

———. "La arquitectura de las novelas de Agustín Yáñez." In *Homenaje a Agustín Yáñez,* edited by Helmy F. Giacoman. New York: Las Américas Publishing, 1973.

———. *The Spanish American Novel: A Twentieth-Century Survey.* Austin: University of Texas Press, 1975.

Callan, Richard. *Miguel Angel Asturias.* Boston: Twayne, 1970.

Carpentier, Alejo. *El reino de este mundo.* Havana: Bolsilibros Union, 1964,.

Chamberlain, Bobby J. *Jorge Amado.* Boston: Twayne, 1984.

Colas, Santiago. *Postmodernity in Latin America: the Argentine Paradigm.* Durham, N.C.: Duke University Press, 1994.

Donoso, José. *Historia personal del Boom.* Barcelona: Anagrama, 1972.

Ellison, Fred. *Brazil's New Novel.* Berkeley: University of California Press, 1954.

Flasher, John J. *México contemporáneo en las novelas de Agustín Yáñez.* Mexico City: Editorial Porrúa, 1969.

Franco, Jean. "Apuntes sobre la crítica feminista y la literatura hispanoamericana." *Hispamérica* 15 (December 1986): 31–43.

Giacoman, Helmy F. *Homenaje a Miguel Angel Asturias.* New York: Las Americas Publishing, 1971.

González Echevarría, Roberto. *Alejo Carpentier: The Pilgrim at Home.* Ithaca, N.Y.: Cornell University Press, 1977.

———. "Alejo Carpentier." In *Modern Latin American Fiction Writers.* Vol. 113, *Dictionary of Literary Biography.* Detroit: Gale Research Inc., 1992.

———. *Celestina's Brood: Continuities of the Baroque in Spanish and Latin American Literature.* Durham, N.C.: Duke University Press, 1993.

Hutcheon, Linda. *A Poetics of Postmodernism: History, Theory, Fiction.* New York: Routledge, 1988.

———. *The Politics of Postmodernism.* New York: Routledge, 1989.

Jencks, Charles. *What Is Postmodernism?* London: Academy Editions; New York: St. Martin's, 1986.

Kadir, Djelal. *Juan Carlos Onetti.* Boston: Twayne, 1977.

Lemos de Oliveira, Celso. *Understanding Graciliano Ramos.* Columbia: University of South Carolina Press, 1988.

Lindstrom, Naomi. *Twentieth-Century Spanish American Fiction.* Austin: University of Texas Press, 1994.

Lyotard, Jean Francois. *The Postmodern Condition: A Report on Knowledge.* Vol. 10, *Theory and History of Literature.* Minneapolis: University of Minnesota Press, 1989.

Martin, Gerald. *Journeys through the Labyrinth: Latin American Fiction of the Twentieth Century.* London: Verso, 1989.

Martínez, José Luis. *Agustín Yáñez.* Guadalajara: Universidad de Guadalajara, 1984.

Mazzara, Richard A. *Graciliano Ramos.* New York: Twayne, 1974.

McCrobbie, Angela. *Postmodernism and Popular Culture.* New York: Routledge, 1994.

McMurray, George. *Spanish American Writing since 1941.* New York: Ungar, 1987.

Menton, Seymour. *Magic Realism Rediscovered, 1918–1981.* Philadelphia: Art Alliance Press, 1983.

Muller Bergh, Klaus, ed. *Asedios a Alejo Carpentier.* Santiago: Editorial Universitaria, 1972.

Ong, Walter. *Orality and Literacy: The Technologizing of the Word.* London: Methuen, 1982.

Oviedo, Jose Miguel. *Mario Vargas Llosa: la invención de una realidad.* Barcelona: Seix Barral, 1970.

Parkinson Zamora, Lois, and Wendy B. Faris, eds. *Magical Realism: Theory, History, Community.* Durham, N.C.: Duke University Press, 1995.

Paz, Octavio. *Poesía en movimiento: México 1915–1966.* Mexico City: Siglo XXI Editores, 1966.

Rodríguez Alcalá, Hugo. In *Asedios a Alejo Carpentier,* edited by Klaus Muller Bergh. Santiago: Editorial Universitaria, 1972.

Sommers, Joseph. *After the Storm: Landmarks of the Modern Mexican Novel.* Albuquerque: University of New Mexico Press, 1968.

Souza, Raymond D. *Major Cuban Novelists.* Columbia: University of Missouri Press, 1976.

———. *The Poetic Fiction of José Lezama Lima.* Columbia: University of Missouri Press, 1983.

Tittler, Jonathan. *Narrative Irony in the Contemporary Spanish American Novel.* Ithaca, N.Y.: Cornell University Press, 1984.

Unruh, Vicky. *Latin American Vanguards: The Art of Contentious Encounters.* Berkeley: University of California Press, 1994.

Williams, Raymond Leslie. *Mario Vargas Llosa.* New York: Ungar, 1977.

———. *Gabriel García Márquez.* Boston: G. K. Hall, 1984.

———.*The Postmodern Novel in Latin America.* New York: St. Martin's, 1995.

———. *The Writings of Carlos Fuentes.* Austin: University of Texas Press, 1996.

Yáñez, Agustín. *After the Storm: Landmarks of the Modern Mexican Novel.* Albuquerque: University of New Mexico Press, 1968.

# Index

# The Author

Raymond Leslie Williams is Professor of Latin American literature and chairman of the Department of Hispanic Studies at the University of California, Riverside. He has published several books and numerous articles on Latin American literature, including *The Writings of Carlos Fuentes* (1996), *The Postmodern Novel in Latin America* (1995), and *The Colombian Novel, 1844–1987* (1991). He is on the editorial board for several journals, including *Hispania* and *Revista de Estudios Hispánicos*. He has also held teaching positions at the University of Chicago and Washington University in St. Louis.

# The Editor

Herbert Sussman is professor of English at Northeastern University. His publications in Victorian literature include *Victorian Masculinites: Manhood and Masculine Poetics in Early Victorian Literature and Art; Fact into Figure: Typology in Carlyle, Ruskin, and the Pre-Raphaelite Brotherhood;* and *Victorians and the Machine: The Literary Response to Technology.*